# THE GOOD PARENT EDUCATOR

## WHAT EVERY PARENT SHOULD KNOW ABOUT THEIR CHILDREN'S EDUCATION

Lee Elliot Major

**First published 2021**

by John Catt Educational Ltd,
15 Riduna Park, Station Road,
Melton, Woodbridge IP12 1QT

Tel: +44 (0) 1394 389850
Email: enquiries@johncatt.com
Website: www.johncatt.com

**ISBN: 978 1 913622 72 5**

Set and designed by John Catt Educational Limited

# Testimonials

Empowering parents with evidence based information on what's important and what works in education is a huge and largely untapped opportunity. This excellent book does exactly that. It answers many of the questions we all have about how best to help and support our children as they make their way through school. It is clear, practical and informative. Every household should have a copy!

**Fiona Forbes, co-founder, Sept For Schools**

The Good Parent Educator is a really useful guide, companion and source of sound advice for parents and carers everywhere. Each highly accessible chapter offers an insightful yet grounded view of the various elements of education and beyond. This handy reference book provides parents with clarity and shares authentic authority on a number of complex and sometimes illusive aspects of education, ensuring everything is navigable by parents and their children alike.

**Susie Weaver, Executive Principal, Cabot Learning Federation**

Whilst most high-stakes jobs come with years of training and a detailed manual, parents receive very little independent guidance when it comes to making choices for their children. The education landscape is constantly shifting, and becoming more granular. It's no longer useful to reflect on our own school experience because, as our children are delighted to tell us, everything's different now.

This book is an indispensable manual for parents navigating the UK school system. He takes a balanced and healthy approach to schooling that enables parents to support and advocate for the children with confidence.

**Julia Silver, author of Tutoring is Not Plan B.**

The Good Parent Educator is an invaluable handbook for all parents. The range of education choices open to parents can be daunting: Lee's book will help you pick your way through the maze with confidence.

**Nick Turpin, Deputy Head teacher and Inclusion Lead, St John's Upper Holloway CE Primary School**

A valuable summary of relevant education research for parents. Covers a range of issues from feedback to private tutoring and the ever escalating educational arms race. Accessible and easy to read, but it doesn't pull any punches in terms of the issues and challenges.

**Steve Higgins, Professor of Education at Durham University**

This book is brilliant at explaining the best known evidence around many of the decisions we have to make as parents. I shared this book with my wife and a few chapters with my teenage daughter when we were talking through the importance of revision, so it really is a book to help with the many difficult choices we face as a parent. Highly recommended and an enjoyable read.

**Dr Wayne Harrison, Co-Founder, WhatWorked Education**

# Acknowledgements

Much of this book is based on the work of other researchers, far too many to mention individually. Research by psychologists, sociologists, economists and educationalists has shone a light on one of the most important activities humans engage in. It's thanks to their endeavours that we know so much about education.

I owe much to two former co-authors who are world leaders in their fields. Steve Higgins showed me the power but also limitations of evidence. Steve Machin produced the hard data showing the rise in parental investments in education – what we termed the escalating education arms race. Thanks also to Jennie Weiner who provided frank feedback (the best kind) and Sandra McNally and Alice Sullivan for comments on specific chapters.

This book also owes much to the insights I picked up from so many generous colleagues during my career, including 12 years at the Sutton Trust, where I worked closely with universities, schools, researchers and teachers, and a decade as a trustee of the Education Endowment Foundation.

I'm grateful to several friends who found time to read over drafts of the book. Many are experts in their own right and parents themselves. They included: Jon Beard, Martin Brammer, Millie Carr, Nicholas Cheffings, Fiona Forbes, Wayne Harrison, Tristram Kenton, Kerra Maddern, Julia Silver, Tim Smith, Nick Turpin, Patrick Wall, Susie Weaver, Ani Martirossian and Trevor Woodhouse. Their comments vastly improved the core advice offered in the book.

Thanks to Alex Sharratt and Jonathan Barnes at John Catt Educational for their encouraging words and wise advice. It was such a relief to work with such a good editor in Harriet Power.

Last but not least I would like to thank my family. This book turned into something much more personal than I first envisaged. My partner and children allowed me to divulge the ups and downs in our own educational journeys. It's one thing to put up with a dad who devotes lots of time to research and writing; it's quite another to become the subject of his work! Without them this book would quite literally not have been possible.

# Contents

1. Navigating the ever-escalating educational arms race .........................9
2. The good parent educator.........................21
3. Helping your children to read.........................35
4. Choosing a school: what really matters......................... 43
5. Mind matters: motivating learning.........................51
6. Homework .........................57
7. Arts and sports.........................63
8. Safeguarding summer-born children .........................71
9. Private tutors .........................79
10. Revision strategies: thinking hard or thinking lazy?.........................87
11. Helicopter awareness of learning .........................95
12. Mind matters: managing cognitive load .........................101
13. Academic selection .........................107
14. Digital dilemmas.........................115
15. Seeking feedback......................... 123
16. Mind matters: learning styles and other myths.........................131
17. Exploring apprenticeships.........................137
18. Choosing a university degree.........................143
19. Debunking Oxbridge myths .........................151
20. Life skills for job hunting... .........................159
21. What's fair game?.........................167
22. The good parent educator quiz.........................175

# 1. Navigating the ever-escalating educational arms race

**Did you know?**

Between the late 1980s and 2005, the time mothers spent on education activities with their children went up from 8 hours to 14 hours a week.

**Key takeaways**

- Despite mounting pressures on parents, there is little authoritative advice to guide them on education.
- You will spend as much as 10,000 days helping your children to prepare for adult life.
- Focusing on effective uses of your time will lead to better outcomes and a more balanced life.

## Becoming a parent

I've been meaning to write this book for 18 years. I know when the first flicker of the idea came to me: 10.43am on 11 August 2003. It was a day that everything changed – the day I became a parent. If only I had known then what I'm about to tell you now.

Two days before our first child was born, we moved into our first home. We were blissfully unaware of whether there was a school in the area, let alone whether it was deemed to be a good one. A light bulb switches on when you become a parent, revealing a new world to which you were completely blind before.

Nothing prepares you for the educational rollercoaster ride of parenthood. I've written books summarising thousands of education studies, advised thousands of teachers, and sat through thousands of hours of school governor meetings. But it's different when you're responsible for navigating the development of your own offspring.

Within 18 months we had two children. Over the next 18 years we experienced the many twists and turns of their educational journeys. From tiny toddlers to terrible teenagers, there've been testing times and tricky moments. And a few triumphs along the way as well.

I can still remember dropping off our children for their first days of school as if it was yesterday. For each of them it was such a momentous and emotional day: their first baby steps towards independence. The crisp autumnal air always signals for me the excitement of the start of another academic year. The rhythms of the school calendar would dictate our lives for the next 20 years.[1]

Like all battle-hardened parents, we have many war stories to tell. There was that heart-stopping phone call from the headteacher who casually informed us that a pupil had tried to stab our son in the eye with a pencil (it narrowly missed). There was that science teacher who, during an infamous parent–teacher evening, confided in us that our 12-year-old son had learned nothing for a whole year because a few disruptive pupils had made the class unmanageable (why hadn't this been dealt with earlier?). There was the episode when our daughter was unceremoniously dropped from the top maths class for no apparent reason other than the teacher didn't seem to like her (she went on to do very well in the subject). And there was the dawning realisation that we should have got our son tested for attention deficit disorder years before we did so (the diagnosis transformed him).

I'd go through it all again to relive just one of the joyous moments only children can bring us: fighting away the tears at the school ceremony when our son unexpectedly won sportsperson of the year (the only pupil to have volunteered to play for every team); brimming with pride when a beaming teacher told us that our daughter had got the top marks possible in her favourite subject (geography); witnessing all their tiny breakthrough moments.

---

1   Many believe that the long summer break came from the need for children to help farmers with the harvest in centuries gone by. But the practice is more likely to originate from the extended summer holidays required by the Victorian professional classes.

Whether it was applying to schools, choosing subjects or helping with homework, we did the best we could. For our generation of parents there is so much to navigate and so little accessible, authoritative advice to guide us. When I entertained the idea of writing this book to other parents, the positive response was instant and overwhelming. I had not been alone in feeling completely unprepared for one of life's most important tasks.

I've spent a lifetime reading, reviewing and producing studies on education and here I'm going to distil all that I've learned into accessible advice for parents. I hope it will enable you to do the best for your children as they progress through their own educational journeys. The best advice is rooted in hard evidence, and so much of what we think matters in education turns out to be wrong. I've included my personal experiences in this book as a parent myself, but everything I'm going to tell you is backed up by research.

'Often what we think our children might need, isn't what they actually need,' one mother with two young children told me. 'The world has changed a great deal since we were in the education system. Often all that parents see is what the media presents to them. It's hard to unpick fact from fiction and hard to understand (a) what choices our kids have, (b) what choices we as parents have, and (c) what we should do for the best.

'Should we all be employing tutors even though we can't afford it? What should we invest in during the early years? Does it really matter what primary school you go to when they're all ranked as 'good' by Ofsted inspectors? Should we be investing in every sort of extracurricular activity going? Or can we do things that don't require money? Should we be reading 20 books a day to them when they are little? Should I be exposing my 3- and 4-year-olds to lots of different professions as we know that children's stereotypes are set by the time they're 6?'

Changes in family make-up and working life mean that many parents and carers are living precarious lives, stretched to the limit trying to make ends meet while trying to give their children the best start in life. Single parents and blended families are becoming the new normal. At the same time there are more families where both mums and dads are working full time, trying to juggle careers with child-rearing. Children's support networks are more complex in a way that they weren't even 10 years ago. Families face difficult choices.

Parents hear daily about the rising levels of anxiety and depression among children. How can they support their children to enable them to achieve what they want to achieve without harming their wellbeing? Do we have to sacrifice one to achieve the other?

# Home schooling

Many of these questions were catapulted into all our homes when the Covid pandemic struck in the spring of 2020. Millions of parents suddenly faced the daunting challenge of becoming makeshift teachers for their children. Never had so many parents been so involved in their children's education.

We were bombarded with well-intended but wildly varying advice. Some experts suggested that home educators brush up on the basics of neuroscience and learning theories. Others warned that we should not attempt to help with homework tasks we could barely manage ourselves. Some said the safest strategy was to just focus on any small wins our children made.

Others still recommended spending time getting outside and exercising, focusing on slow and mindful breathing, or listening to music. 'If things are going a bit wrong, because your child's tin foil man won't stand up straight or the maths equation is just too difficult and you can't get out of an important Teams meeting to sort everything out, then encourage everyone to just breathe,' one counsellor told *Good Housekeeping* magazine.

Many teachers meanwhile said the most important thing was for families to establish routines to bring structure to the endless days at home. For those of us with teenagers with brains programmed for late nights and mornings, this was easier said than done. Despite being showered with guidance, the experience of home schooling left many parents feeling overwhelmed, stressed and exhausted.

Home schooling had been hell, reported one single mother trying to balance full-time work and helping her 7-year-old son with his homework. A new campaign group for parents, Sept for Schools, said it had been overwhelmed with similar reports from parents across the country, many reduced to tears trying to meet impossible expectations. Schools couldn't re-open soon enough.

One good thing that came out of it all was a growing appreciation among mums and dads of how tough teaching can be.

Covid completely shifted the parent–teacher dynamic. Relationships between schools and families have changed forever. The post-pandemic world of home working and online learning means that the change is permanent. From now on, for good or ill, increasing numbers of parents will want to have more say over their children's education.

One father I know who has two sons at primary school felt strongly that he and his wife knew far more about their sons' specific learning needs than their teachers could ever hope to know. Three months of overseeing their sons' daily lessons had revealed several gaps in their knowledge. One son couldn't articulate the alphabet properly. The other wasn't being stretched on his algebra enough.

Ahead of their parent–teacher meeting, the sons' parents had looked up the curriculum on the school's website, and listed all the areas that needed addressing. This wasn't going to be the usual parent–teacher meeting. These parents were not going to politely nod to whatever the teacher had to say.

## Educational arms race

Not all parents review their children's academic progress in such detail, but many of us are devoting more and more time to help their education. I've found that the pandemic has accelerated trends that I'd already been observing in my own research. In our 2018 book *Social Mobility and Its Enemies*, my co-author Steve Machin and I documented one of the stand-out patterns of modern societies: the ever-escalating educational arms race. In an increasingly competitive and unequal world, we are going to ever-increasing lengths to do the best for our children.

The signs of this arms race are all around us: the tiger parents loitering outside the school gates ready to pounce on unsuspecting teachers; the escalating costs of private tutors and private school fees; and the extortionately high house prices in the neighbourhoods of the most sought-after state schools.

The average time spent by parents on education-oriented interactions has steadily risen in the UK. Between the late 1980s and 2005, the time mothers spent on child-rearing activities went up from 8 hours a week to 14 hours a week. Over the same period, the time fathers spent with their children went up from 4 hours a week to 6 hours a week. This extra time was spent on a range of activities, from reading to children to helping them with their homework.

Studies also reveal a rising tide in enrichment: the endless ferrying of children to music lessons and sports training; frog-marching them to visits of museums and galleries; taking holidays to expose them to different cultures and enhance their personal CVs. If you haven't got the inclination or cash to keep up in this race, your children will be left behind.

The use of private tutors has boomed. The percentage of children aged between 11 and 16 in England receiving private or home tuition rose by over a third in a decade, increasing from 18% in 2005 to 25% by 2016. And in England, London has become the capital of private tutoring, with 40% of 11- to 16-year-olds receiving support. England though has some way to go to match South Korea, where spending by households on private tutoring now rivals public-sector education budgets. Private tutoring has become a multi-billion-dollar global industry that is growing exponentially.

The educational arms race in the UK is characterised by a stark social divide. Research I'm involved in has shown that children in middle-class homes are much more likely to be helped by their parents, spend time on homework and benefit from private tutoring.

The school–home boundary has become completely blurred. In my work with teachers I've also noticed schools are doing ever more for their poorest pupils, from providing meals to identifying health issues to safeguarding against any harm. Many are acting as hubs of social welfare as much as centres of learning.

For many parents, investing in their children's future is now a lifetime's commitment. University professors, to their horror, now have to greet queues of parents turning up alongside sons and daughters during university open days. A generation ago this was strictly a student affair – if it happened at all.

Moving from an elite to mass higher-education system has meant two things: more people going to university and parents having to pay tuition fees. We shop in a university marketplace. Many parents hover over their children's choice of not just undergraduate but postgraduate degrees as well. As customers, we want to know if another year of study is money well spent.

Grandparents are getting in on the act too. When time-poor parents are at the height of their busy careers, time-rich grandparents can step in to help with child-rearing duties, bringing them to school and helping with their schoolwork. The grey pound can make a big difference to the education prospects of grandchildren by paying for private tutoring or school fees.

Boomerang children meanwhile come bouncing back to home after studying at university. This isn't through choice: they just can't afford rents elsewhere. This would have been unheard of a generation back. In 2017, the Office for National Statistics found that 37% of men aged 18 to 34 in the UK lived with their parents. The bank of mum and dad has developed a new dedicated offshoot: the job-hunting support service. Parents are getting more involved in interview preparation, internship searches and up-skilling of their stuck-at-home adult offspring.

With each generation, the stakes get higher. In the past, advantage was found through A-levels and university degrees; today it is achieved through postgraduate degrees and exclusive internships in prestigious firms. A degree is no longer the automatic passport to a well-paid job it once was; now a particularly exclusive degree plus a master's qualification is often required.

Inevitably the educational arms race has exposed parenting's dark side. In the UK, a significant minority of parents admit to cheating in school admissions: buying a second home, or renting a property nearby (see chapter 21). Some admit to completing their children's assignments. Others pay for doctors to diagnose medical conditions so their children can gain extra time in exams or secure a coveted school place ahead of someone else's child.[2] As far as we know, bribing university admissions tutors and paying others to do your children's tests has not reached this side of the Atlantic – yet.

What is driving all this tireless activity? We are to some extent responding to the environment in which we find ourselves. In a world of shrinking opportunities and high rewards from success, the educational arms race is fuelled by our primal instincts to do the best for our children's futures.

We are living in unprecedented times. Children growing up today have the unfortunate distinction of being the first generation since the war to face worse prospects than their forebears. Their earnings in real terms will be less on average than those of their parents. They are less able to afford to rent or buy a house. Decent jobs are harder to come by. And those jobs are bereft of the benefits once deemed standard fare: guaranteed pensions, health insurance and sabbaticals.

Is it any wonder we are witnessing worryingly high levels of anxiety and depression, and insatiable demand for meditation and mindfulness exercises? Perhaps all our sweat and tears is driven by unconscious intergenerational guilt: the generous and unsustainable benefits enjoyed by previous generations have stored up problems for today's generations.

If the post-war period was the golden era of social mobility, the post-pandemic world is likely to be a dark era of declining opportunity. Those who climbed the social ladder in previous generations don't want their children to slip back down the rungs. The spectre of downward mobility hangs over many families. The pandemic strengthened powerful trends already in train; growing gaps between richer and poorer parents, the unstoppable rise of computer technology in the workplace, and an increasingly global market in jobs have all made it much harder to obtain a decent standard of living for all.

Getting an education is of course much more than a path to making money. But it remains the golden ticket to higher wages. In recent decades, people with degrees have seen their earnings pull further ahead of non-graduates. But this average conceals wide variations in the salaries associated with different university courses. A degree from Oxbridge in particular and elite Russell group universities in general may confer a much bigger pay advantage than other degrees on average. But many other university degree courses are still worth considering (see chapter 18). And many apprenticeships also lead to healthy wage packets. Meanwhile, failing to get basic GCSEs at age 16 incurs a bigger penalty in working life than for previous generations.

---

2    It can also bring a financial advantage through a disability living allowance.

This is a race that pits parents against each other: what matters is how much better your children's grades are than those they are competing against. That's what counts if you want to win a place at a selective sixth form college or prestigious university or sought-after internship. Education policies stressing choice and competition in schools further encourage sharp-elbowed behaviour.

But the good parent educator understands that education is far more than just grades. The inexorable rise of A grades and first-class degrees has ironically put an extra premium on the non-academic characteristics that distinguish the stand-out job candidates from the rest. Studies suggest that our children will need to communicate, network and be resilient – very resilient – to prosper in the workplace of the future.

This book will prompt you to reflect on what you think education is for. There isn't a simple answer. Experts have debated the role of schools for as long as we have educated children. The answer you get depends on who you ask.[3] My view is that education is much more than about maximising students' test scores. I believe that learning is useful for learning's sake. Ultimately, education is about nurturing children into independent thinkers ready to enjoy and understand the world around them.

## More harm than good?

By the time your children finally leave the nest, you may have spent as many as 10,000 days thinking and worrying about their every step towards independent life in the big wide world – not to mention hundreds of sleepless nights.[4]

The big question we all need to face up to – and the reason for writing this book – is this: how do we ensure our efforts are actually having a positive impact? The problem is that one of the most important jobs we try to do is largely a hit and miss affair. But just stumbling through blindly and hoping it will help isn't good enough.

Time and time again we shall find that what we assume matters in education is wrong. You may be making matters worse. But let me also make one thing clear: this book is not a guide for how you can replace your teacher. We need to leave teaching to the trained professionals.

---

3   One of the best films and plays highlighting the competing views of what education is for – learning for learning's sake or maximising students' test scores – is Alan Bennett's *The History Boys*. Centred on Cutlers' Grammar School, Sheffield, a fictional boys' grammar school, the play pokes fun at the headmaster's lofty aspirations for getting his pupils into Oxbridge. Some of the teachers at Cutlers believe that education is much more than just grades.

4   Increasing numbers of children now live with their parents into their late twenties or early thirties. 10,000 days equates to around 27 years.

What I will offer you are the best tips, taken from the best evidence available, to better navigate the twists and turns of your children's educational journeys. This book provides the information to empower parents from all backgrounds to engage with teachers in more meaningful and beneficial ways.

At the same time, in writing this, I've drawn on my own experiences and knowledge both as education expert but also as a flawed parent. In home life there is a yawning gap between theory and reality. Much of the guidance represents an impossibly high bar for parents to aspire to. If you manage to take on just two or three tips, I believe they can still make a difference.

By focusing more on effective uses of the limited time you have available, I hope it will lead to more balanced living as well. I've come to believe that we are increasingly in danger of doing more harm than good – for both us and our children.

I know so many parents who are leading hectic, stressed-out lives. They are trying to live up to impossible expectations for their children while managing the pressures of their careers and jobs. It's like being on a constant treadmill while spinning plates and juggling balls all at the same time. Something has to give; often it is relationships with partners that are ruined in the process.

I've seen many marriages fall apart when children leave for university or college (only for them to return home afterwards as job-seeking graduates). Parents spend their lives preparing their children to fly off. They then don't know what to do when they're gone. The empty nest syndrome can destabilise the whole family.

So much of us goes into our children that we risk losing the things that brought us together in the first place. With eyes fixed on other horizons, all that is left of the vessel we first embarked on is a sad, empty hulk.

We need to be ever watchful that this project doesn't become more about us than our children. I'm sure I'm not the only one to harbour deep suspicions of fellow parents who dominate dinner parties boring everyone with endless stories of what their sons or daughters have achieved. It's as if they are using their children to grab a second chance for the glory that evaded them in their own lives. This is all about their own status.

One mother at our local school professed to me that her son was her lifetime's work. Her son was clearly a talented boy. But it became clear that whatever he accomplished was the result of a combined family effort, whether it was winning the annual egg race, getting top marks in the maths quiz, or performing a piano concerto in front of all of the school.

Another father developed an obsession with his daughter's football prospects. He became convinced she could make it to the top. He seemed to spend every hour ferrying her to weekend matches and evening training sessions. After years of toil, he was left heartbroken when his daughter lost interest and said she wanted to spend more time with her friends.

Difficult as it is for parents, there is a time when we have to let go. Our children get good grades for themselves, not for you. As we shall see, an aim of teaching and learning is to nurture our children so they can learn and think independently. Excessive parenting isn't good for our children's self-reliance and self-esteem.

But what do we know about different types of parenting? And how can education research help us as parents? It is these crucial questions I turn to in the next chapter.

# References and reading

9.   *Did you know?*: Doepke, M. and Zilibotti, F. (2019) *The economic roots of helicopter parenting.* Phi Delta Kappan.

12.  *'If things are going a bit wrong'*: Sutton, M. (2021) 'Experts share their advice on coping with the stresses of home schooling', *Good Housekeeping*, 11 January.

12.  *'Home schooling had been hell'*: Sellgren, K. (2020) 'Coronavirus: home-schooling has been hell, say parents', *BBC News*, 8 July.

13.  *Time spent on child-rearing activities*: Doepke, M. and Zilibotti, F. (2019) *The economic roots of helicopter parenting.* Phi Delta Kappan.

13.  *The percentage of children receiving private tuition rose by over a third*: Kirby, P. (2016) *Shadow schooling: private tuition and social mobility in the UK.* The Sutton Trust.

13.  *Spending on private tutoring in South Korea*: Elliot Major, L. and Weiner, J. (2020) 'Rethinking social mobility in education: looking through the lens of professional capital', *Journal of Professional Capital and Community.*

13.  *Middle-class children are more likely to benefit from private tutoring*: Elliot Major, L., Eyles, A. and Machin, S. (2021) *Unequal learning and labour market losses in the crisis: consequences for social mobility,* CEP Discussion Papers dp1748, Centre for Economic Performance, LSE.

14.  *37% of men lived with their parents*: Office for National Statistics (2019) *Milestones: journeying into adulthood.*

14.  *Parents admit to cheating*: Elliot Major, L. and Machin, S. (2018) *Social mobility and its enemies.* Penguin.

15.  *Children today face worse prospects than their forebears*: Elliot Major, L., and Machin, S. (2020) *What do we know and what should we do about social mobility?* SAGE Publishing.

15.  *People with degrees earn more*: Elliot Major, L. and Machin, S. (2018) *Social mobility and its enemies.* Penguin.

15   *Failing to get basic GCSEs incurs a bigger penalty*: Machin, S., McNally, S. and Ruiz-Valenzuela, J. (2020) 'Entry through the narrow door: the costs of just failing high stakes exams', *Journal of Public Economics*, 190, 104224.

16.  *Skills needed to prosper in the workplace of the future*: Gutman, L. M. and Schoon, I. (2013) *The impact of non-cognitive skills on outcomes for young people. A literature review.* Education Endowment Foundation/Cabinet Office.

# 2. The good parent educator

**Did you know?**

Teaching is one of the most complex, challenging and demanding activities that our species has ever invented.

**Key takeaways**

- Excessive parenting may be doing more harm than good for us and our children.
- We need to look beyond parenting advice to evidence-informed education tips to help our children's development.
- The good parent educator empowers their children through education.

## Fucking them up?

Could our efforts to do the best for our children unwittingly be fucking them up? Many parenting experts seem to think so. A vast literature of parenting advice has flourished amid ever more manic parenting behaviour. Authors claim that intensive parenting does more harm than good. It isn't healthy for us, or our kids.

Reading these books, I'm reminded of the poet Philip Larkin's oft-quoted words: 'They fuck you up, your mum and dad. They may not mean to, but they do.' We have apparently produced a generation of entitled young people incapable of coping with everyday life. We face an epidemic of depression and mental anxiety.

Books urge us to take an alternative path and break free from overparenting. This could all be avoided 'if parents would just take a giant step back, check their ambitions at the door, and do what's really best for their kids'. Our aim should be to foster self-sufficient children.

Over the last 50 years, parents have been classified into several different species as if we were a family of the animal kingdom. In British society, it is said, you can distinguish everyone's social class as soon as you enter a room; well, at school drop-off time, you can classify every parent type as soon as the school gates are in sight.

Helicopter parents, for example, hover over every move their son or daughter makes. They are obsessively involved in every education decision, from choosing a school to considering what university degree to take.

Helicopter wings evolved alongside the rise of mobile phones in the 1990s – 'the world's longest umbilical cord'. In the 1980s when I went to university I didn't contact my mum for two months. Now some parents are worried if they don't receive hourly updates from their children. Before the 1990s, it was unusual, not to say unsettling, to see parents on campus. Now university professors are faced with busloads on university open days, armed with lists of detailed questions about their children's academic options.

Tiger parents are a related but distinct species. They adopt a strict, disciplinarian approach to child-rearing. The Asian American academic Amy Chua first advocated this parenting style in her 2011 book *Battle Hymn of the Tiger Mother*. The tiger parent's goal in life is to maximise their children's talents: ferrying them to football games or musical performances, and scheduling tutoring sessions or extra weekend classes. They are driven by a neurosis that no matter what they have done, it is never quite enough.

'Neurosis underpinned every conversation, as most of us had the same goal of getting our children into the same selective schools,' Tanith Carey, a self-proclaimed tiger mum, told *The Telegraph*. 'Then there was the depressing cloak-and-dagger secrecy and paranoia because we all lived with the constant fear that other mothers were doing more than we were.'

The British variety of the brasher American and Asian species is more panther-like, going to great lengths to conceal the extra coaching their children receive. The aim is to leave the impression that their sons and daughters are naturally brilliant. Packs of them lurk outside the school gates.

In our book *Social Mobility and Its Enemies*, my co-author Stephen Machin and I documented another type of parent: the sharp-elbowed warrior. These parents will stop at nothing in the fierce battles over school admissions. The most ruthless will cheat to get their children ahead: renting flats nearby schools just before admission deadlines, or suddenly rediscovering their religious beliefs at church so their offspring are guaranteed a place at the local faith school (see chapter 21).

Over the last half a century, psychologists who study people's behaviour have developed their own classifications. The idea of parenting styles was first introduced by the American psychologist Diana Baumrind. They have been evolving ever since. Authoritative parents encourage children to be responsible for their actions and to think for themselves. Authoritarian parents threaten to punish their children if their orders aren't obeyed. Permissive parents are warm and supportive, but reluctant to enforce any rules at home. Uninvolved parents don't do much at all.

Studies suggest that children from authoritative families are more successful at school and in later life. Poorer outcomes are associated with other parenting styles – authoritarian, permissive or uninvolved. Having at least one authoritative parent is a good thing, even if the other parent demonstrates a different style. (Contrary to what you might think, parents don't always have to aspire to a united front. Different parenting styles can complement each other.)

The actions of authoritative parents are similar to what the American sociologist Annette Lareau calls 'concerted cultivation'. Children are urged to contribute to family discussion over the dinner table and encouraged to seek feedback from their teacher if they receive poor grades on their homework. Lareau observed this behaviour mainly among middle-class families.

Lareau argues these efforts are preparing children for middle-class adulthood: knowing how to challenge authority and work the system, and presumably maturing into sharp-elbowed parents themselves. In contrast, the working-class parents Lareau observed practised what she terms 'natural growth parenting'. They allowed their children to enjoy unstructured time, and gave them orders rather than soliciting opinions. But as any teacher will tell you, these are generalisations: parental styles vary enormously among parents of all social classes.

## What parent type are you?

| Parenting style | Telltale |
| --- | --- |
| Helicopter | Hovering over their every education decision |
| Tiger | Ferrying them to football games or musical performances |
| Sharp-elbowed warrior | Jumping the school admissions queue |
| Authoritative | Encouraging them to think for themselves |
| Authoritarian | Ensuring orders are obeyed |
| Permissive | Enforcing no rules |
| Uninvolved | Not doing much at all |
| Good educator | Empowering them through education |

# Parenting problems

The kingdom of parenting styles is fascinating, prompting us to reflect on what our own style is. But it's less clear how practically useful it is. How do you change your parenting style? How can you take on proven ways of aiding your children's learning?

Distinct parenting types are also constructs we've made up. Most parents are a combination of styles, a blend of authoritarianism and authoritativeness, part tiger, part permissive parent. Your inclinations can depend on the time, place and what mood you're in.

The link between parents being involved with their children and their children's success at school is well established. Parents are the single biggest predictor of children's life outcomes. Yet it's proved very difficult to develop successful programmes that get parents to be more involved with their children to the benefit of their learning. It's hard to change lifelong habits by the time you've become a parent.

It's refreshing to know that even the world's most successful people find parenting to be one of life's biggest challenges. 'With each generation they're making parenting harder, they're making the bar crazier, like, for what a parent is supposed to do,' Michelle Obama has said. 'Here we come with all the rules and all the guidebooks, and we still feel unprepared.'

Like all species, we are also profoundly shaped by what is around us. The American economists Matthias Doepke and Fabrizio Zilibotti have shown that in countries with large earnings gaps between the rich and poor, parents push harder to ensure their children have a path to security and success. Economic incentives, in their view, have transformed the hands-off parenting of the 1960s and 1970s into the frantic, over-scheduled activity we witness in the early 21st century.

The economists conclude that the only way to address the epidemic of hyper-competitive and over-involved parenting is to reduce the huge income gaps between the rich and poor – hardly a straightforward task. But it's hard for parents to take a step back and ignore these powerful incentives shaped by our external environment.

The answer for parents I believe is to look beyond parenting advice to what we know about education. If we can better understand what matters for our children's development then we can support our children's learning in a healthy and balanced way. What's more, for the first time we now have evidence-informed tips available that can help transform excessive parenting into effective learning.

# Education home truths

I'm astonished by how many of my good friends (and experts in their own fields) believe they know what's best in the classroom. Most have never been anywhere near a teacher training college or education seminar – let alone stepped in front of a group of pupils. They would never expect people to jump to conclusions about their own profession.

Perhaps it's because teaching is such a big part of all of our lives. We've all sat in a classroom. Yet our memories of teaching are unreliably distant. They relate to an ancient world, unrecognisable compared to current classroom climates. Would we assume we could do the work of surgeons or High Court barristers? Perhaps it highlights the tragic lack of status of teachers in our society.

My first lesson for you is to not presume you know how to teach, or what matters most for learning – unless you are a professionally trained teacher. One silver lining of the Covid pandemic has been a greater appreciation of this noblest of professions. After the first few idyllic days of home learning in 2020, parents discovered how tough it can be. By the end of a gruelling week many were tearing their hair out. The reality of what it takes to teach had literally hit home.

The more I understand about teaching and learning, the more I marvel at its complexity. I've worked with experts to summarise the best education studies from across the world. Great teaching is nothing short of a human wonder. The American educational psychologist Lee Shulman put it best, writing that 'classroom teaching … is perhaps the most complex, most challenging, and most demanding, subtle, nuanced, and frightening activity that our species has ever invented'. It is part science and part art. It is a unique experience between teachers and learners, a dance they play out in one classroom at one point in time.

There is no basic replicable recipe for effective classroom teaching. The best definition is that great teaching is simply that which leads to greater student progress. It helps to know a subject well enough so you can instantly recognise students' common mistakes. Good teachers are also masters of instruction, questioning, stimulating, offering model answers and gradually introducing new ideas. They also have to deal with 30 or more children with different needs, moods, triggers, personalities, and interest levels. They provide the safety and security for children to know it's okay to get things wrong.

But other than this, it is hard to pin down. Two equally great teachers may adopt completely different approaches. And expert observers are as likely to disagree as agree on whether they have witnessed great classroom practice. If they find it hard to spot, then us amateurs stand little chance.

For parents there are two further 'must knows'. Firstly, classroom teaching is by far the most important factor within schools for children's learning and wellbeing (see chapter 4). This may seem blindingly obvious. But most education-talk is wasted on so many other things – what types of schools your children attend, whether they are grouped into academic sets, whether or not they wear uniform, how much homework and marking they get. In the scheme of things, these are distractions in comparison to the quality of classroom teaching. Education's challenge can be reduced down to one simple question: how can we make the interactions between teachers and their classrooms of pupils as effective as possible?

Secondly, the quality of classroom teaching varies enormously within every school, whether it is Eton or Hogwarts or the local academy or comp.[5] We obsess about which school our children will attend. But the much more important question is which teacher will our children be taught by? (See chapter 4).

## Age of enlightenment

The good news is that during the last decade, schools have experienced a revolution in the use of research. Classroom teachers digest academic reports and pour over data-sheets in ways that just didn't happen 10 years ago. We are lucky to be living in an enlightened era.

It would be wrong to think of this as pure science – there are just too many things happening in a room filled with 30 young minds. My friend and co-author Steve Higgins has done a lot to bring evidence into the teaching profession. And Steve is always careful to talk about best bets in the classroom, not certainties.

In 2010, we first worked together on the Pupil Premium Toolkit. Published by the Sutton Trust charity, this was the first ever Which?-style guide for teachers, summarising thousands of studies into easily digestible headlines. The aim was to help teachers boost the progress of poorer pupils. This eventually morphed into the snappily titled Education Endowment Foundation Teaching and Learning Toolkit. You can access it freely on the EEF's website today. The guide has been used by hundreds of thousands of teachers across the world from the UK to Spain, Australia and Latin America. In 2019, Steve and I published our award-winning *What Works?* book. This drew out common principles for teachers, alongside tips for classroom practice.

The evidence-informed movement in education has flourished. Thousands of teachers now write daily in dizzying detail about the nuances of their classroom

---

5    We make exactly the same mistake with barbers and hairdressers. There is usually a wide variation in the quality of different hairdressers in the same salon.

practice, across all subjects and phases of education, covering a multitude of research topics, from brain science to learning theory. Many are social media stars and government tzars.

But for parents, many of these wise words are buried beneath the jargon of education. If you don't know your standard deviations from your metacognitive strategies, you'll struggle to digest them.

A recent fad among teachers, for example, is to wax lyrical about cognitive load theory (see chapter 12). This theory suggests that our working memory can only juggle a few chunks of information at any one time. We shouldn't overload children with too much information at once. Teachers have always intuitively understood this. Finding a theory that backs up intuition can be useful. But throwing around scientific-sounding terms can also be alienating for outsiders (and in this case going against the very principles of the theory itself).

The aim of this book is to translate educational wisdom into accessible tips for parents. As we get ever more engaged with our children's learning, what should we understand and what can we ignore? I'd like to think I'm opening a gate into education's secret garden.

But be warned: this is a landscape full of surprise turns, dead-ends and hidden pot-holes. Much of this book is devoted to debunking common myths and misconceptions. What really matters in education will challenge some previously held assumptions.

We praise our children far too much, for example (see chapter 15). The urge to congratulate them for the smallest of achievements is irresistible for most parents. This, after all, is affirmation for us as much as them. But studies suggest that excessive praise can be harmful to learning. Being praised for an easy task sends a subliminal message of low expectations. Praise sparingly so it's valued. It's more helpful if you can reward them for their effort and hard work (see chapter 5).

Meanwhile, many of the things we think are important for our children's schooling aren't. Homework during primary school years has little impact on children's development (see chapter 6). Receiving marks from teachers for assignments are useless for children unless they are given specific instructions on what they need to do next. And by the way, school results are mostly a reflection of the children who attend in the first place, not the school itself.

Getting into the top academic sets, meanwhile, isn't necessarily the best thing for your son or daughter (see chapter 13). Extra tutoring can help children. But too much risks children falling into a dependency mindset. And hours spent re-reading and highlighting texts isn't much help for revising for exams. You need to work your brains by testing yourself (see chapter 10).

It is just as important to know what hasn't worked in education. Teaching is prone to falsehoods and passing fads. The most dangerous myths endure because they have a scientific ring of truth to them – even if this ring is an empty promise. For non-experts it's easy to fall under their spell.

I've been told about 'learning styles' so many times I've lost the will to smile politely in response. I've heard it from people who are successful in business, teachers and most alarmingly from children themselves. It is widely believed that classifying children as visual, auditory or 'kinaesthetic' learners can help them. Yet the research could not be clearer: there are no benefits from this approach. There is a real danger with this. Children's progress can be limited if they are labelled as a particular type of learner (see chapter 16).

Being evidence-informed is also about knowing what we don't know. This book is all about adopting this approach: to seek robust, impartial and independent research to challenge our prior views and expose our gaps in knowledge. Former US Secretary of Defense Donald Rumsfeld was much maligned when, ahead of the Iraq War in 2002, he explained that there are 'known unknowns, but also unknown unknowns'. But he had a point. 'I know that I know nothing,' is how the Greek philosopher Socrates put it 2,400 years before, at least according to Plato. True wisdom comes to us when we realise how little we understand.

Steve Higgins likes to imagine educational knowledge as a medieval map of the world, where some areas are better known than others. We know a lot about the best ways of learning to read, for example. But large swathes of the educational territory have yet to be explored. And some bits never will be. There are no randomised control studies showing how we can improve the prospects for summer-born children or how to maximise your chances in an Oxbridge interview.

Great strides have been made in the science of learning in recent years. But these are baby steps compared with the progress made by the physical and medical sciences. Humans are refreshingly hard to predict. In education, this means we have to tread carefully.

This book is also a very personal one. I've scoured the shelves of the world's academic libraries. But I've turned to experts and tapped into my own experiences when offering advice as well. They are my best bets for you to consider. Some bits of advice will work for your child, others will not. This is one of the golden rules of learning. For all the general evidence we have amassed, every human relationship is different. You will have to see what works for you and your children. And what works one day won't always work.

## Not just grades

Most parents care more about the wellbeing of their children than their children's test scores. They have good reason to do so. Life is much more than academic grades. Being mentally and physically healthy is important in itself. But it also has educational benefits.

Eating better, sleeping well and being fit in body and mind are essential for healthier learning. It is also true that teenagers' brains are programmed to sleep and wake later than their parents. This may seem like laziness. But it's biology! Better sleep can improve concentration and behaviour in the classroom.

Healthy eating lowers the risk of major illnesses and stress, and can boost self-esteem and sleep quality. Food should be low in sugar, salt and fat – and needn't be expensive. Studies show that the act of sitting down with your children regularly over dinner is a powerful predictor of better outcomes in adulthood. We don't know whether this is just a sign of good family relationships, or due to healthy eating, or because of something else entirely.

Go for a walk with your children: it is good exercise for the body and brain. I've found it can change the dynamic with teenage sons and daughters. The fresh air and open space somehow prompts them to open up in ways unimaginable back at home. The trick is to let them do the talking!

In his influential work, Nobel Prize-winning economist James Heckman argues that academic skills are mostly shaped before the age of 10, while personality skills – such as sticking at tasks, getting on with other people and being self-confident – are malleable through adolescence and into early adulthood. Parents play a powerful role in improving these non-academic skills. And they are equally important in determining life prospects.

Playing sports and participating in the arts have important educational value in themselves (see chapter 7). They are associated with increased self-confidence and wellbeing, improved social interaction and leadership skills. In my view, children should spend as much time on these as their academic study.

## The good parent educator

In the crowded kingdom of parents, how would you spot the good parent educator?

They are in awe of the miracles performed in the classroom. But they can confidently and constructively challenge schools over their children's learning. They understand the power but also limitations of research. They are rightly sceptical about the many fads, myths and magic bullets that will come their way.

Like authoritative parents, they try to find the right balance between discipline and freedom for their children. This is less helicopter parenting, more helicopter learning: enabling children to take ownership and find the bird's eye view of their own learning. They are not so much sharp-elbowed, as even-handed. They know and love their children for who they are, not what they want them to be.

It's unlikely that any mortal being could live up to these impossibly high expectations, of course. I hope this book offers a realistic way forward, providing practical tips for the twists and turns of your own children's journeys. I'm acutely aware of the realities of family life and how hard it can be for parents. It's not easy to create independent learners ready to prosper in the world. It takes a lot of work and effort.

Parents shouldn't expect everything to go right. Most things turn out to be okay in the end. Amid mounting pressures, this message is something that parents don't hear enough.

This book is packed full of advice, amassed from hundreds of studies. Each chapter is dedicated to an important education topic. They are arranged in rough chronological order, from pre-school to post-graduation. Each section includes key takeaway messages and five nuggets of advice, as well as suggestions for extra reading.

In later chapters, considering apprenticeships and university applications, I offer advice for the young adults making these choices. Parents should be taking a step back, providing helpful guidance and suggestions, not making decisions for them. This is about being an authoritative parent and getting them to think for themselves.

At the end of the book you can take a quiz to check your own understanding. This isn't a make-or-break test that you can pass or fail; it's a way of consolidating what's been covered. You don't necessarily need to know everything in one go; each chapter is a self-contained summary; each piece of advice covers a separate point.

You can pick and choose what tips work for you. There are many simple things that can help your children that don't require lots of time and money. My aim is to offer insights into the insider knowledge that too few parents are aware of, not to add yet further pressures in their busy lives.

I've used the generic terms 'parents' or 'mums and dads' throughout the text. But the advice of course applies to all parents: carers, foster parents, adoptive parents, single parents, same-sex parents, grandparents. These are universal issues whatever the family set-up may happen to be.

## 2. The good parent educator

If you aspire to be a good parent educator, the most important thing to remember is that you are trying to empower your children through education. You should know when to provide support, but also when to let go. Learning comes from failing as well as succeeding. As Yoda, the wise mentor in the *Star Wars* movies, says: 'The greatest teacher, failure is.'

# References and reading

21.   *Philip Larkin*: Larkin, P. (1971) 'This be the verse'.

21.   '*if parents would just take a giant step back*': Glass, G. and Tabatsky, D. (2014) *The overparenting epidemic*. Simon & Schuster.

22.   '*the world's longest umbilical cord*': Childs, M. (2016) 'Mullendore: cell phone is umbilical cord for helicopter parents'. University of Georgia website.

22.   '*Amy Chua first advocated this parenting style*': Chua, A. (2011) *Battle hymn of the tiger mother*. Bloomsbury.

22.   '*Neurosis underpinned every conversation*': Carey, T. (2016) 'I was a tiger mum, but I've learnt the error of my ways', *The Telegraph*, 12 September.

22.   *The sharp-elbowed warrior*: Elliot Major, L. and Machin, S. (2018) *Social mobility and its enemies*. Penguin.

23.   *Psychologists have developed their own classifications*: Dewar, G. (2018) *Parenting styles: an evidence-based, cross-cultural guide*. Parenting Science website.

23.   '*first introduced by the American psychologist Diana Baumrind*': Baumrind, D. (1966) 'Effects of authoritative parental control on child behavior', *Child Development*, 37 (4), pp.887–907.

23.   *Children from authoritative families are more successful*: Chan, T. W. and Koo, A. (2010) 'Parenting styles and youth outcomes in the UK', *European Sociological Review*, 27 (3), pp.385–399.

See also: Dornbusch, S. M., Ritter, P. L., Liederman, P. H., Roberts, D. F. and Fraleigh, M. J. (1987), 'The relation of parenting style to adolescent school performance', *Child Development*, 58 (5), pp.1244–1257.

23.   '*concerted cultivation*': Lareau, A. (2002) 'Invisible inequality: social class and childrearing in black families and white families', *American Sociological Review*, 67 (5), pp.747–776.

24.   '*With each generation they're making parenting harder*': Kappler, M. (2020) '9 parenting tips from Michelle Obama and her mom', *Huffington Post*, 17 September.

24.   *In countries with large earnings gaps, parents push harder*: Doepke, M. and Zilibotti, F. (2019) *Love, money, and parenting: how economics explains the way we raise our kids*. Princeton University Press.

25. *'classroom teaching … is perhaps the most complex':* Shulman, L. (2004) *The wisdom of practice: essays on teaching, learning and learning to teach.* Jossey-Bass.

25. *Great teaching is that which leads to greater student progress:* Coe, R., Aloisi, C., Higgins, S. and Elliot Major, L. (2014) *What makes great teaching?* The Sutton Trust.

25. *'it is hard to pin down':* Brown, et al. (2001) *Magic bullets or chimeras? Searching for factors characterising effective teachers and effective teaching in numeracy,* BERA annual conference.

26. *The Pupil Premium Toolkit:* Higgins, S., Kokotsaki, D. and Coe, R. (2011) *Toolkit of strategies to improve learning: summary for schools spending the Pupil Premium.* The Sutton Trust.

26. *Education Endowment Foundation Teaching and Learning Toolkit:* Higgins, S., Katsipataki, M., Coleman, R., Henderson, P., Major, L. E., Coe, R. and Mason, D. (2015) *The Sutton Trust–Education Endowment Foundation Teaching and Learning Toolkit.* Education Endowment Foundation.

26. *'our award-winning What Works? book':* Elliot Major, L. and Higgins, S. (2019) *What works? Research and evidence for successful teaching.* Bloomsbury.

28. *Imagining educational knowledge as a medieval map of the world:* Higgins, S. (2018) *Improving learning: meta-analysis of intervention research in education.* Cambridge University Press.

29. *Sleeping well is essential for healthier learning:* Dewald, J. F., Meijer, A. M., Oort, F. J., Kerkhof, G. A. and Bögels, S. M. (2010) 'The influence of sleep quality, sleep duration and sleepiness on school performance in children and adolescents: a meta-analytic review', *Sleep Medicine Reviews,* 14 (3), pp.179–189.

29. *Eating dinner together is a powerful predictor of better outcomes:* Putnam, R. D. (2000) 'Bowling alone: America's declining social capital', in Crothers, L. and Lockhart, C. (eds.) *Culture and politics,* pp.223–234. Palgrave Macmillan.

29. *Personality skills are malleable:* Heckman, J. and Mosso, S. (2014) 'The economics of human development and social mobility', *Annual Review of Economics,* 6 (1), pp.689–733.

# 3. Helping your children to read

**Did you know?**

Reading for pleasure is more important for children's development than whether their mum or dad have a university degree.

**Key takeaways**
- Children who are read to regularly by their parents do better at school.
- There are no magic ways to create a love of reading in children when it's not there to begin with.
- Getting your children to read for 20 minutes a day will help them to develop reading skills needed for learning and life.

## A pleasing discovery

Professor Alice Sullivan was interested in how our knowledge of words changes over our lifetimes. She decided to get a group of 42-year-olds to repeat a vocabulary test they had first undertaken when they were 16. Just as an after-thought, she also decided to look at their reading habits when they were young children. That decision led to an amazing discovery.

Alice oversees one of the treasure troves of British social science: a national study that tracks the lives of 17,000 people from around the country born in one week in 1970. The British Cohort Study (BCS70) is special because it collects incredibly rich details about its participants. Studies have been able to look at how everything from medical histories to school results to social class backgrounds affect their lives. It's the scientific equivalent of the popular *Up* TV series that has interviewed 14 people every 7 years since they were 7 years old in 1964.

To her surprise, Alice found children who read for pleasure received huge benefits from it. This is reading you do for its own sake, not something forced on you for homework or by someone else.

Children who were motivated to read books did far better in academic tests than those who read less regularly, even though these children came from similar homes. Children who were read to regularly by their parents from the age of 5 also performed better than other children.

And that's not all: independent readers made significant gains in vocabulary and spelling, but also in maths as well. Being able to read enables children to absorb and understand new information in all subjects. Reading for pleasure was found to be more important for children's development than whether their mum or dad had a university degree.

'It was quite serendipitous that we found the enormous impact that reading for pleasure had on learning in childhood,' Alice told me in 2020 when I had the privilege of hosting a podcast series to celebrate the 50th anniversary of BCS70. It's not often researchers stumble upon such a clear-cut finding.

One reason why reading is so powerful is that books introduce a far richer vocabulary of words and phrases than normal conversations with adults. The more demanding the fiction is, the bigger the vocabulary gains are. 'The power of reading is a deeper kind of learning,' Alice said. 'I think people do understand that learning is more than just being crammed for a test.' Deeper reading habits improve children's lives.

What the research tells us, primary school teachers know instinctively. They see it every year, when 5-year-old toddlers step through their gates for the first time. Ask a headteacher what one thing parents should do to help their children before they begin school and they are very likely to give the same answer: parents should sit down and read with their children and try to instil a love of reading.

## Reading's big dilemma

But here's the catch. How do you create a love of reading in children when it's not there to begin with? This is one of the biggest dilemmas in education. We know an awful lot about developing reading skills among pupils. It's one of most fruitful fields of education research. But knowing how to read is one thing; waiting to devour your next novel is another.

Over the years I've seen schools, teachers and parents struggle to instil a love of reading in their children. One nationally lauded headteacher tried every trick and approach to get his own sons into the reading habit, but to no avail. As a governor of an all-boys school, the lack of reading among our pupils was a constant concern, in a world of growing online distractions and instant gratifications.

International surveys show that British children read less than children in many other countries. Shockingly, around 25–30% of children leave school at age 16 unable to read or write properly.

As a parent, I've learned that you have to have realistic expectations about encouraging your children to read for pleasure. For some of your children it will feel like something they were always meant to do. But for others you'll feel like you're knocking your head against the wall.

What you can aim for is helping to improve the reading levels of your children. They may not all become book lovers, but they should be able to understand and engage with text when needed. Learning to read is one the most powerful skills we learn – some say it's the most important task that teachers have. It is important because it enables children to read to learn. It's a foundational skill needed to prosper in education and in the world.

# What you can do

## Start at the beginning

One of the guiding principles of education is to start as early as possible so you don't have to catch up later. From the moment your child is born, you should talk to them. Tell them what you're up to, what's on your mind. Try to use simple, short sentences. Sing to them, or read out rhymes. It all helps; they will pick up the basics of language even before they are able to speak themselves.

When they are able to speak, get them to explain their experiences or describe things or tell stories. Children's development of speaking skills will help them to learn to read and write.

Reading to your children in the early years helps them to get used to the rules of reading – following words from left to right and top to bottom, for example. Running your finger under words as you read will help them understand that words have meaning, and familiarise them with the sounds and rhythms of stories.

## 20-minute rule

Establish a daily routine for your children's reading during their primary school years. I recommend this should last for 20 minutes. Any less than this, and the benefits diminish dramatically. One American study found that children who read 20 minutes per day were exposed to well over a million words a year, and were more likely to do well in tests.

In the early years it's good for children to read aloud. You can ask questions before, during, and after reading. But you need to judge this carefully: some children are put off if they feel it is becoming yet more homework. It helps if you can convey a love of literature yourself. Read to them. It should be fun.

Try to avoid reading becoming a deadening box-ticking exercise. When our children were younger we had to complete a weekly reading record for the school. This just leads to panic on Sunday evenings before the record had to be handed in on Monday morning.

Children can tell if your heart isn't in it. One father told me that when he was tired he tried to speed read books by missing chunks out. His sons always stopped him, saying, 'Dad, you missed a bit.'

Many parents find that having an evening routine can work well: meal, bath, reading, bed.

## Let them choose

Children need to be empowered, not forced, to read. You're not going to like all their literary choices. It may be more David Walliams than Roald Dahl. Their pleasure might not be yours. One study found that when children were asked which book they had enjoyed most, 80% said it was one they had chosen themselves. The experts recommend high-quality texts. Reading fiction seems to be particularly good for improving reading skills. But be pragmatic. Any reading is better than no reading at all.

How you read with children is as important as how frequently you read with them. Encourage them to be the teller of the story. Listen and ask questions. In education this is called dialogic reading.

## Variety of reading

We tried everything with our children: buying comic books and graphic novels which offer less text and more pictures; getting them to listen to audiobooks (or podcasts); encouraging them to watch film or TV versions of books; and taking them to the local theatre.

Look for reading opportunities in everyday life: going through recipes together from cooking books; reading maps when going on a journey; or sharing newspapers and magazines.

The research suggests that reading on the internet is not as beneficial as reading from paper. This is likely to be due to the different nature of content children engage with online. Spending all their time watching videos doesn't help!

## Phonics

Explore phonics with your children before they start their Reception class. Phonics is the method used by teachers to introduce pupils to the sounds letters make (phonemes). Children then learn how to piece those letters together to make words. This is like cracking the code of written words, and it is called decoding. It is the most reliable way we know for getting young children to learn how to read words. Research suggests phonics is particularly beneficial for 4- to 7-year-olds. It's most effective when delivered by qualified teachers, but you can still help.

Ask your local schools what particular phonics approaches they are following, and buy the book which will provide a step-by-step guide. Remember though that phonics is only one literacy strategy among many that teachers use: older children may be struggling to read because they don't know enough words yet or they don't understand what they are reading (in teacher-speak they lack vocabulary or comprehension). Older learners who continue to struggle may also have other specific language needs such as dyslexia. Get them diagnosed and get extra help.

## Work with teachers

Work in partnership with your child's teachers so you can complement what they are doing in class. Is the teacher reading aloud daily to their class? What classroom strategies are they using for improving decoding, vocabulary and comprehension?

Teachers are always making finely balanced judgements. Too little challenge in texts means little learning for pupils, but too much can make it overwhelming.

Are there any materials for parents? Learning to read is one of a few areas of schooling backed up by thousands of studies. The school should have clear answers.

## Librarians

Finally, talk to the school librarian if your children are fortunate enough to be at a school that has one. School librarians can be inspiring. Sadly not all schools have a library, but librarians at public libraries can also be a great source of recommendations.

**Five bits of advice**

- Talk to your children from the moment they are born – it all helps to develop their language skills.
- Establish a daily routine of 20 minutes for your children's reading.
- Let them choose their books – any reading is better than no reading at all.
- Take your children to the library, and make sure you have lots of books at home, whether bought or borrowed.
- Explore phonics with your children before they start school.

# Reading and references

If I could recommend one thing to read it would be:

*Reading 101: a guide for parents* by Reading Rockets, available on the National Educational Association website.

This is a useful guide from the United States with lots of tips for parents to understand what it takes to learn to read (and write), and how parents can help young children grow as readers, writers and learners. There are also updated blogs and news articles on a range of literacy topics.

## References

35.   *Did you know?*: Sullivan, A. and Brown, M. (2015) 'Reading for pleasure and progress in vocabulary and mathematics', *British Educational Research Journal*, 41 (6), pp.971–991.

35.   *Alice oversees a national study*: The 1970 British Cohort Study, Centre for Longitudinal Studies, UCL Social Research Institute.

36.   *Up* TV series: Solazzo, C. (2019) *The story behind TV's longest-running documentary series, Up*. Royal Television Society.

36.   *Children who read for pleasure receive huge benefits*: Sullivan, A. and Brown, M. (2015) 'Reading for pleasure and progress in vocabulary and mathematics', *British Educational Research Journal*, 41 (6), pp.971–991.

      See also: Sullivan, A. and Brown, M. (2015) 'Vocabulary from adolescence to middle age', *Longitudinal and Life Course Studies*, 6 (2), pp.173–189.

      Sullivan, A., Moulton, V. and Fitzsimons, E. (2021) 'The intergenerational transmission of language skill', *The British Journal of Sociology*, 72 (2), pp.207–232.

37.   *British children read less*: Department for Education (2012) *Research evidence on reading for pleasure (education standards research team)*.

37.   *25–30% of children leave school unable to read or write properly*: Elliot Major, L. and Machin, S. (2018) *Social mobility and its enemies*. Penguin.

38.   *'One American study'*: Nagy, W. and Herman, P. A. (1987) 'Breadth and depth of vocabulary knowledge: implications for acquisition and instruction', in McKeown, M. and Curtis, M. (eds.) *The nature of vocabulary acquisition*, pp.19–59. Erlbaum.

38.   *'80% said it was one they had chosen themselves'*: Department for Education (2012) *Research evidence on reading for pleasure (education standards research team)*.

38.  *Reading fiction is good for improving reading skills*: Jerrim, J. and Moss, G. (2019) 'The link between fiction and teenagers' reading skills: international evidence from the OECD PISA study', *British Educational Research Journal*, 45 (1), pp.181–200.

39.  *'reading on the internet is not as beneficial'*: Delgado, P., Vargas, C., Ackerman, R. and Salmerón, L. (2018) 'Don't throw away your printed books: a meta-analysis on the effects of reading media on reading comprehension', *Educational Research Review*, 25, pp.23–38.

39.  *Phonics is particularly beneficial for 4- to 7-year-olds when delivered by qualified teachers*: Elliot Major, L. and Higgins, S. (2019) *What works? Research and evidence for successful teaching*. Bloomsbury.

## Other general references for this chapter

Bus, A. G., van IJzendoorn, M. H. and Pellegrini, A. D. (1995) 'Joint book reading makes for success in learning to read: a meta-analysis on intergenerational transmission of literacy', *Review of Educational Research*, 65, pp.1–21.

Castles, A., Rastle, K. and Nation, K. (2018) 'Ending the reading wars: reading acquisition from novice to expert', *Psychological Science in the Public Interest*, 19, pp.5–51.

Logan J., Justice L., Yumuş M. and Chaparro-Moreno L. (2019) 'When children are not read to at home: the million word gap', *Journal of Developmental & Behavioral Pediatrics*, 40 (5), pp.383–386.

Quigley, A. (2020) *Closing the reading gap*. Routledge.

Schwartz, S. and Sparks, S. (2019) 'How do kids learn to read? What the science says', *Education Week*.

Snowling, M. J. and Hulme, C. (2007) *The science of reading: a handbook*. Wiley Blackwell.

# 4. Choosing a school: what really matters

**Did you know?**
Most of the variation in children's school results is due to what happens outside, not inside, the school gates.

**Key takeaways**
- It's very hard to put your finger on what makes a school good.
- Treat league tables with care: they should primarily be used to prompt questions when visiting schools.
- Quality of teaching is far more important than other school features such as class sizes or school uniforms.

## Back to school

We are sitting in a packed school auditorium and I'm being scolded by my partner for looking around too much. There's a buzz of growing anticipation among the parents as we wait for the school head to appear. We are told to turn off our phones. A respectful silence descends across the room.

It's funny how we all retrogress to being children again when we go back to school. Perhaps it is the distinctive smell of school halls that transports us back in time, or the way that teachers command a room. The 50-year-old CEO behind me nervously asks if there is time to use the bathroom.

But this evening is about our children, not us. And like all 11-year-olds, our sons and daughters are already acting like fully formed teenagers: fidgeting in their chairs, wanting to be anywhere else but here. Yet we are making a decision that could shape their lives for the next seven years. Before we know it, we are whisked away by a smartly dressed pupil and taken on a dizzying tour of crowded classrooms, corridors and computer labs. When we get home, we fall into our armchairs exhausted. Only four more schools to visit.

I've witnessed so much poor decision-making by parents (including myself) during countless school visits over the years. Otherwise sensible, well-balanced adults suddenly make silly, uninformed decisions. School choices are based on rushed impressions, bad assumptions and second-hand suppositions.

To be fair to parents, it's very hard to put your finger on what makes a school good. Some believe their success is down to immaculate school uniforms or military-style discipline; others are impressed with shiny new buildings or glitzy dance studios. But these are little more than hunches: none of them are backed up by hard evidence.

Studies show schools that give more homework get better results. But what we don't know is whether the results could be due to something else the schools are doing rather than setting homework itself. Does homework lead to better results, or are high-achieving pupils simply doing more homework?

I've always felt that a school's effectiveness comes down to the headteacher setting a tone throughout the school. But studies have also struggled to single out a 'headteacher effect'. Some highly experienced teachers claim they can just smell a good school as soon as they walk through the door. We pick up on the most basic of signals: is the phone answered promptly; are the toilets in good condition?

However, there are some things the evidence can tell us about. Parents should know about the widespread myths around school choice. They need to be armed with the right questions when considering what matters most for their children's future schooling.

## Debunking myths

Perhaps the biggest myth is that a child's academic grades will be mostly determined by the school they attend. If school A has 100% of children achieving 5 GCSEs including English and maths, and school B has only 50% meeting this benchmark, then school A must be twice as good as school B, right?

Well, actually no. One of the unassailable findings from research is that most of the variation in children's school results is due to individual and family characteristics outside the school gates, not what happens inside them.

It's devilishly hard to disentangle the factors outside and inside schools that contribute to our children's academic grades years into the future. But just to give you an idea of how much schools contribute, consider their impact on final GCSE grades at age 16. An average pupil going to the very best performing school in the country instead of the worst performing one would improve his or her results by one grade for each GCSE exam they take.

There are important caveats to this finding. Some schools can, and do, have a bigger impact than others: they produce better academic results despite very similar intakes of pupils. It is also true that in an increasingly competitive education race, one extra grade at GCSE can make all the difference: for example whether your son or daughter gets into a selective sixth form college.

But the evidence is clear: if you can provide a stable and supportive home background for your children, they will fulfil their academic potential at most schools they attend. Hopefully this knowledge will make the whole question of which school you choose just a little less stressful.

## School uniforms – threadbare claims

Some headteachers still claim that having school uniforms improves results. Uniforms have some benefits. They remove competition and comparisons between students over the latest fashions. Yet there are no reputable studies that conclude that introducing a school uniform will, by itself, improve the academic results, behaviour or attendance of pupils. For every school that has succeeded in raising attainment by introducing a uniform policy, another has failed. The research, you could say, is threadbare.

## Class sizes

Reducing class sizes by a few pupils is a popular policy advocated by politicians. But these changes have little impact. It may seem obvious that reducing the number of pupils in a class will improve the quality of classroom teaching. But the research suggests it is hard for teachers to change what they do unless the class is very small (say, 15 pupils). Teachers tell me that teaching a class of 20 pupils feels very different to teaching a class of 30 pupils; the children seem more relaxed and more sure of getting some attention if they need it.

But in terms of improving results, a school would be better off investing in extra teachers or teaching assistants for one-to-one or small-group teaching.

## Ask about the best teachers

We know that the quality of classroom teaching matters most for children. It also varies a lot in every school, where there will be great teaching alongside teaching that needs improving. Teachers have a huge impact on us. They can inspire a lifelong passion for a subject, or a deep hatred for it that you never recover from. In every school across the land there are inspirational teachers and teachers who need to improve their practice.

A fundamental question for any school is whether they know who their best teachers are. If they do, moreover, how are they using their best teachers to improve teaching elsewhere in the school? Which teachers need extra development, and what is the school doing to support this? What is the school's record on retaining its best teachers?

## Ask about setting

Grouping children by perceived ability doesn't work well in most schools because it is implemented poorly (see chapter 13). Poorer children and those born in the summer tend to be put into bottom sets irrespective of their academic potential. Teachers and their pupils fall into a fixed mindset, with little subsequent movement of pupils between sets. And setting detracts from the bigger question of how good classroom teaching is across the school.

Ask the school what evidence they have that the setting arrangements are more effective than mixed-ability classes. Why do they set in maths and not in English? (There is no evidence that supports this.) How often do they reappraise which pupils are in different sets?

## League tables – treat with care

Numbers in official print assume an authority that is illusory when you dig beneath the surface. In our busy and complex world, simple statistics retain an irresistible power. I should know: I created the first university guide for *The Guardian* newspaper. Knowing the dark arts of league tables, my advice is to treat them with care.

League tables can be misleading in many ways. As discussed above, they wrongly suggest that academic results are mainly the product of the schools themselves, which is not true. They also only provide a historical picture of achievement, relating to children who started at the school five or seven years previously. And they only capture a small aspect of what schools are doing.

But league tables are a good prompt for asking schools questions. Parents can now look at a wealth of government data available for individual schools, showing progress for different groups of pupils. And inspection reports can provide useful context alongside these figures – as long as they have been published recently. Even a cursory look at these sources will prompt some challenging questions.

Why has the progress of pupils not improved over the last three years, for example? What percentage of pupils are meeting expected national standards in exams? How does the progress of pupils at the school compare with those at other schools with similar initial intakes of pupils?

But there are also many other questions you should consider when choosing a school. What does the school offer in arts and sports? What is the provision for special educational needs? How does the school deal with disruptive behaviour in the classroom? What are the exclusion rates? What is the turnover of teachers? What do current pupils think?

## Beware hothouses

Finally, remember that high-achieving schools aren't for everyone. Many parents find out too late that their children aren't suited to the academic hothouses they're having a thoroughly miserable time in. I've seen the tragedy play out many times. Huge efforts are made to provide extra tutoring support to get their son or daughter into a prestigious academic school. They then spend years stuck at the bottom of the class. This can undermine their sense of worth and create a lifetime's guilt over failing to meet their parent's unrealistic expectations.

I've also seen many parents pleasantly surprised that their local community school has good teachers offering strong pastoral care which helps bring out the best in their pupils. The question you must ask is what school is right for your son or daughter. That's not necessarily the same thing as which school is ranked highest in the league table.

## Moving schools

Some parents ask about when it's right to pull your child out of a school. If your son or daughter is deeply unhappy, or you feel the school isn't working for them, should you try elsewhere? For many children and their parents, leaving a school can be a traumatic experience. For others it's a much-needed fresh start.

From an education perspective, stability in the classroom as well as the home is generally a good thing for children. For this reason I would advise careful consideration before moving your child to a different school. Ask yourself whether the issue is about them or the school. Have you done all you can to help the situation?

What are the views of your teacher and headteacher? If you have exhausted all the possibilities, and it's still not working, then a move may be the best thing.

Remember that teachers are also human beings. They're not perfect and they don't have all the answers (and they aren't withholding them from you). Sometimes they're having a bad day – or year. One mum once helped her son through a year with a grumpy teacher by saying 'maybe he forgets to eat breakfast in the morning'. It helps to tell your child that it's not their fault.

**Five bits of advice**

- Class sizes and school uniforms don't matter as much as you might think.
- Ask the school how they are using their best teachers to improve teaching across all classrooms.
- Ask teachers how often pupils are moved up and down academic sets.
- Use league tables and other information as prompts to ask questions about the school.
- Remember that high-achieving schools aren't for everyone.

# Reading and references

If I could recommend one thing to read it would be:

Coe, R., Aloisi, C., Higgins, S. and Elliot Major, L. (2014) *What makes great teaching?* The Sutton Trust.

This review of research aims to answer the seemingly simple question of what makes great teaching.

Defining effective teaching is not easy. But we do know that teachers need a good knowledge of their subject and strong instructional skills. The report concludes that student progress is the yardstick by which teacher quality should be assessed: 'Ultimately, for a judgement about whether teaching is effective to be seen as trustworthy, it must be checked against the progress being made by students.'

## References

43. *Did you know?*: Elliot Major, L. and Machin, S. (2018) *Social mobility and its enemies.* Penguin.

   See also: Hanushek, E. (2016) 'What matters for student achievement', *Education Next.*

44. *Schools that give more homework get better results*: Elliot Major, L. and Higgins, S. (2019) *What works? Research and evidence for successful teaching.* Bloomsbury.

44. *Children's school results are due to individual and family circumstances*: Elliot Major, L. and Machin, S. (2018) *Social mobility and its enemies.* Penguin.

   See also: Hanushek, E. (2016) 'What matters for student achievement', *Education Next.*

45. *'it is hard for teachers to change what they do unless the class is very small'*: Elliot Major, L. and Higgins, S. (2019) *What works? Research and evidence for successful teaching.* Bloomsbury.

   See also: Boden, A., Archwamety, T. and McFarland, M. (2000), 'Programmed instruction in secondary education: a meta-analysis of the impact of class size on its effectiveness', paper presented at the Annual Meeting of the National Association of School Psychologists (New Orleans, LA, 28 March – 1 April 2000).

   See also: Nye, B., Hedges, L. V. and Konstantopoulos, S. (2002) 'Do low-achieving students benefit more from small classes? Evidence from the Tennessee class size experiment', *Educational Evaluation and Policy Analysis*, 24 (3), pp.201–217.

46.    '*the quality of classroom teaching matters most*': Hanushek, E. (2016) 'What matters for student achievement', *Education Next.*

46.    *League tables relate to children who started at the school five or seven years previously*: Leckie, G. and Goldstein, H. (2009) 'The limitations of using school league tables to inform school choice', *J. R. Statist. Soc. A*, 172, pp.835–851.

# 5. Mind matters: motivating learning

**Did you know?**
Studies have found that students with a growth mindset do better in tests than equally talented students with a fixed mindset.

**Key takeaway**
- Using the tried and tested techniques of sports coaching can improve your children's learning.

## Growth mindset

It's easy to feel sceptical about the power of positive thinking promoted by the world's sporting elites.

'I know that if I set my mind to do something, even if people are saying I can't do it, I will achieve it,' David Beckham has said. Beckham wasn't the most naturally gifted of footballers. Yet he ended up playing for his country over 100 times. He became a global icon and now co-owns a football club. Not bad for a boy who came from Leytonstone, a working-class area in East London.

The greatest basketball player of all time, Michael Jordan, has a similar inspirational message. 'I've missed more than nine thousand shots. I've lost almost three hundred games,' he says in an advert for his sponsor Nike. 'Twenty-six times, I've been trusted to take the game-winning shot, and missed, and that is why I succeed.' Jordan didn't make it into his college team, and was initially rejected by professional teams.

I sometimes wonder how helpful it is to use such incredible one-off success stories. There's a sneaking suspicion that the Beckhams and Jordans of the world are blessed with innate talents alongside their impressive work ethic. But I've become convinced that what we call a 'growth mindset' in education can help us all to develop our talents whatever they are. Many children have a miserable time when it comes to sport in school. But we can learn a lot from competitive sports when trying to improve our children's learning.

The theory of growth mindset was developed by Carol Dweck, a psychologist based at Stanford University in the United States. Dweck's insights came after studying the contrasting attitudes towards failure among a group of students. Students could be classified as having a fixed mindset or a growth mindset. Fixed mindset learners believe that people are born with certain abilities and talents, and that these can't be changed. Growth mindset learners, on the other hand, believe that abilities and talents can be improved through effort and hard work. Dweck found that equally talented students did better in tests if they had a growth mindset.

I've always been struck when watching sport that people value effort over raw talent.[6] Loyal fans will turn a blind eye to pretty much everything apart from their players giving up. They love the players who work the hardest on the playing field. In elite sports where everyone is technically gifted, it's mental drive that distinguishes the winners from the losers. The most tired sports clichés are all about effort: 'we gave a 120%'; 'we left it all out there on the pitch'.

Often it's not the most talented young footballers who make it from academies into the professional game. It's those who have some talent, but who are also motivated and disciplined enough to work hard to improve their game. The best players may make it look effortless on the sports field. But hours of dedicated practice has gone on behind the scenes.

It's odd that in the classroom we fall instead into the trap of a fixed mindset. Some children are seen as naturally better than others academically. Of course we are born with different talents. But so much progress at school is due to years of sustained support provided by families outside the classroom.

---

6    I used to take my son to watch his favourite football team, Arsenal, at their home stadium in North London. At the time they were managed by Arsène Wenger and were renowned for beautiful, flowing football. Yet even at the Emirates stadium, the biggest roars were reserved for players running tirelessly for their team.

Sports players can provide powerful role models for children. The central lesson is that if you work hard and improve your own personal bests, you can succeed in life. As one teacher told me, 'it isn't about being best, it's about making your best efforts'. You can only focus on what you can control, not what your competitors can do. Focusing on other people takes away from your own efforts, making you fall further behind.

These principles should apply just as well to the exam hall as the sports arena. But attempts to get teachers and pupils to embrace a growth mindset in classrooms have struggled to replicate the gains observed by Dweck in earlier studies. One of the main implications of Dweck's work is that it is better to praise effort rather than accomplishment. But it turns out that it isn't a simple matter of telling children to try harder.

For parents there are some important bits of advice. Praise your children's efforts only if those efforts have achieved good results. If they are getting things wrong, then urge them to explore other options. Telling a child they 'did their best' or 'just keep trying' can make them feel dejected. It may move them towards a fixed mindset. How many times have you heard a child say they're just not good at a subject?

Good teachers see effort and success in one area and remind their pupils of this to help them sustain effort in another area they are finding more difficult.

Failure, meanwhile, should be seen as a learning opportunity. It can be hard to see it this way. But making mistakes is a vital part of the learning process at any age.

## Goodhew's law: stretching but realistic goals

Another sporting lesson that can be transplanted to the classroom is setting step-by-step goals. This approach was behind the inspirational story of the British swimmer Duncan Goodhew. Goodhew was the plucky Gold medal winner in the men's 100m breaststroke in the Moscow 1980 Olympic Games.

Swimming had been Goodhew's escape from despair and despondency. He had been bullied at school for going bald after he fell out of a tree. He had also been diagnosed with dyslexia that made him feel stupid compared with his classmates.

But it was Goodhew's training regime that captured my imagination. He had worked hard to improve his swimming times step by step, every time cutting off a few more milliseconds off his best time. These were stretching but realistic goals. It would have been overwhelming if he had thought too much about his ultimate goal of winning an Olympic Gold.[7]

---

7    Many authors adopt a similar incremental approach when writing books, for example by focusing on completing just one page or half an hour of writing at a time.

Goodhew's story highlights another key lesson. You should focus on goals to self-improve, not goals for winning the race or the title. Sports coaches emphasise self-improvement, saying that the titles will then 'look after themselves'.

Your children should look to themselves rather than others when trying to improve their progress. This requires a conscious effort. You are swimming against a strong tide flowing in the opposite direction: a social media world of constant comparisons and a schooling system that places too much emphasis on end-of-year test scores. Children will feel more in control of their learning if they set their own goals. Self-improvement, not external validation, is the route to greater self-esteem.

Children will make more effort if they believe ability is malleable rather than fixed. In education speak, children do better if they are oriented towards mastery, or self-improvement, rather than performance, or how well they do compared with their peers.

Goodhew's story also highlights another lesson from sports coaching: you need to be preoccupied with small, detailed improvements to develop as an athlete. As the educationalist Dylan Wiliam has pointed out in his efforts to help teachers improve feedback to pupils, basketball coaches focus on specifics and avoid vague generalities. 'In helping players improve their free throw percentage, basketball coaches do not just tell the athletes to make sure that they get the ball through the hoop,' says Wiliam. 'They focus on mechanics such as reminding the athlete to bend their knees, and to keep the elbows tucked in.'

Wiliam contrasts this with the feedback often received by pupils in the classroom (see chapter 15). It isn't helpful to tell children that they need to improve their work, even if this is true, he argues. It is more helpful to highlight what kinds of errors they are making, and what they need to do to improve.

**Five bits of advice**

- All children can improve through hard work and effort – it's not about being best but making your best efforts.
- Praise effort, not achievement, but avoid praising ineffective efforts.
- Get your children to focus on improving personally, rather than thinking about others.
- Encourage them to establish stretching but realistic step-by-step goals.
- Children need specific steps to get better.

# Reading and references

If I could recommend one thing to read it would be:

Dweck, C. S. (2017) *Mindset: changing the way you think to fulfil your potential (updated edition)*. Random House.

The central tenet of Carol Dweck's influential work is that you should attribute educational progress to effort rather than innate capability. 'Athletes with the growth mindset find success in doing their best, in learning and improving,' she writes. 'They don't need a prize to feel confident, and instead attain it through adopting a growth mindset and focusing on self-improvement.'

Growth mindset has grown like wildfire in Britain's classrooms. Never has an idea seemed to chime so much with the ideals of teachers. But while the evidence is encouraging, some of Dweck's original studies have failed to show similar effects when replicated by other researchers.

## References

51.    *Did you know?*: Dweck, C. (2017) *Mindset: changing the way you think to fulfil your potential (updated edition)*. Random House.

53.    *'have struggled to replicate the gains observed by Dweck in earlier studies'*: Rienzo, C., Rolfe, H. and Wilkinson, D. (2015) *Changing mindsets evaluation report and executive summary*. Education Endowment Foundation.

53.    *'better to praise effort rather than accomplishment'*: Dweck, C. (1999) 'Caution – praise can be dangerous', *American Educator*.

53.    *'it isn't a simple matter of telling children to try harder'*: Dweck, C. (2016) 'What having a "growth mindset" actually means', *Harvard Business Review*, 13.

54.    *'In helping players improve their free throw* percentage': Wiliam, D. (2011) 'What is assessment for learning?', *Studies in Educational Evaluation*, 37, pp.3–14.

# 6. Homework

**Did you know?**
The amount of effort put in by children is a stronger predictor of future grades than the amount of time spent on homework.

**Key takeaways**
- Homework has little impact at primary school, but can be effective at secondary school if done well.
- Homework can raise stress levels in any family home.
- After years of escalating levels of homework, we are now experiencing a backlash against it.

## Homework scars

Like many parents I bear the scars from homework battles during our children's formative years. We suffered it all: stressed nights struggling to finish our son's paper mache volcano; back-aching hours crouching down to complete a Lego castle; simmering tensions on Sunday evenings helping our daughter draft pointless letters to Queen Victoria.

When I think of homework I think of tensions, tears and tantrums. Homework produces an incendiary mix of emotions guaranteed to raise stress levels in any family home. Parents feel guilty that they aren't doing enough to support their children. Children hate giving up their free time. And a nagging question hangs over everyone: is anyone actually benefiting from all this?

It's no surprise that homework has little impact on children's learning during the primary school years. It's a high-risk learning strategy at the best of times. For a start, there's no qualified teacher present. And modern-day homes are full of distractions. If left unchecked, homework can promote bad learning habits – copying answers, rushing tasks or studying in front of the television. And parents can't resist stepping in to do children's tasks for them.

Over the years, numerous parents have confided in me about their clandestine work. The helping hand of mum and dad can be hard to detect, but it's ever present. Some will even write with their opposite hand so it looks like their younger children's work – anything to just get it done. Some will improve the work, but not too much to be noticed. Needless to say, cheating doesn't have any education value for children, and can add to their feelings of inadequacy. Teachers are also good at spotting it, as they see what is produced in class.

Homework wars have raged over the years: encouraged for one generation of children only to be rejected for the next. One American study found that children are spending twice as much time on homework each day than they did in the 1990s. After years of seemingly escalating levels of homework, we are experiencing another backlash.

More and more primary schools are abandoning homework altogether. In our local primary school, for example, children are now asked to just practise spellings and times tables. Parents and children are much happier. Other schools are limiting homework to an hour a night, two or three nights a week, or banning deadlines that fall on Mondays, or the day after coming back from holidays.

We have to be careful with education comparisons across different countries as the worlds outside the school gates are so different. But it hasn't gone unnoticed that many of the highest performers in the international education league tables are countries that set less, not more, homework. They include Finland, South Korea and Japan, where weekly homework hours are much fewer than those in the UK.[8] In many countries, homework is frowned upon: parents don't think schools should intrude on children's time once the school day is over as they have other things to learn and enjoy. Many countries meanwhile that prioritise homework are among the worst performers in the international education league tables.

But homework for secondary school pupils, if done well, can lead to an extra five months' progress over one academic year. By this time, in theory at least, older pupils have developed more as independent learners. They are able to block out

---

8    Studies comparing countries throw up lots of interesting differences between nations. Children in Finland also don't start school until they are seven years old. The UK meanwhile is characterised by one of the widest gaps in homework hours between wealthy and disadvantaged pupils.

external distractions (like parents who don't have the skills or knowledge to help with more advanced material!). The most effective homework is that which consolidates and complements learning taking place in the school.

However, research on homework suffers from one of those chicken and egg questions that come up a lot in education: we don't know whether it's just high-achieving pupils who are simply doing more homework in the first place, or whether the homework itself is improving academic grades (or both). We also know little about the potential costs of excessive homework on children's wellbeing and happiness and their family relationships.

# What you can do

## The ten-minute rule

A helpful rule of thumb to follow is the 'ten-minute rule'. This recommends a daily maximum of ten minutes of homework for every successive year group. Pupils in their first year of primary school at age five (Year 1), for example, should do no more than ten minutes of homework each night. Sixth formers (Year 12) should do no more than two hours, or 120 minutes.

This advice has held firm over many decades. 'A good way to think about homework is the way you think about medications or dietary supplements,' advises Harris Cooper, the American expert on homework. 'If you take too little, they'll have no effect. If you take too much, they can kill you. If you take the right amount, you'll get better.' All study has diminishing returns. And excessive homework encroaches on valuable time spent on sport, exercise, hobbies or relaxation and family life.

## It's the trying that counts

The amount of effort put in by children, measured by how many of the tasks or questions they attempt, is a stronger predictor of future academic grades than the amount of time spent on homework. This finding is consistent with other education research suggesting that praising children for their hard work is more productive than congratulating them on what they have achieved (see chapter 5). Half an hour of genuine work is better for them than two hours of staring at the screen. Think quality not quantity.

## Sow the seeds of study skills

Homework is an opportunity to nurture study skills – managing time, organising material and weighing up different learning strategies. These skills can be learned (see chapter 11). Good study habits may be one of homework's most powerful lasting benefits.

## Adopt a hands-off approach when they're older

Parents should only play an active role with their children's study at home when they are struggling, particularly during their early years. But you should adopt a hands-off approach when they are doing well in school, particularly during their later years. Remember the whole aim of schooling, and one of the potential benefits of homework, is helping children to become independent, lifelong thinkers and learners.

## Questions for teachers

Are teachers using homework to provide feedback to your children? One study found homework commented on by teachers had twice the impact of homework that was left unmarked. However, comments are only useful if they are acted on by pupils.

Does home learning dovetail with what's happening at school? It should consolidate material covered in past lessons or offer a taster of what is to come. Pupils might need more practice to get better at something, such as reading, or they might need to prepare for something new, such as pre-learning spellings for the next lesson.

What's the school's justification for setting lots of homework? If your primary school is setting lots, then you should challenge the teachers: what evidence do they have that it is benefiting pupils?

### Five bits of advice

- Remember the 'ten-minute rule' – less is more, particularly in the early years.
- Effort exerted is what counts, not hours expended.
- Homework is an opportunity to nurture study skills.
- Ask teachers how homework is complementing what is happening at school.
- Don't do your children's homework for them – it's not good for you or for them.

## Reading and references

If I could recommend one thing to read it would be:

Cooper, H. (2007) *The battle over homework: common ground for administrators, teachers, and parents.* Corwin Press.

In this book, American academic Harris Cooper reviews studies on homework. He urges parents to be positive about homework as this will be the attitude their child acquires. 'Homework is a source of complaint and friction between home and school more often than any other teaching activity,' writes Cooper. 'Parents protest that assignments are too long or too short, too hard or too easy, and too ambiguous … These complaints are not surprising, considering that homework assignments are influenced by more factors than any other instructional strategy.'

## References

57.     *Did you know?*: Elliot Major, L. and Higgins, S. (2019) *What works? Research and evidence for successful teaching.* Bloomsbury.

58.     *Homework has little impact at primary school*: Elliot Major, L. and Higgins, S. (2019) *What works? Research and evidence for successful teaching.* Bloomsbury.

        See also: Farrow, S., Tymms, P. and Henderson, B. (1999) 'Homework and attainment in primary schools', *British Educational Research Journal*, 25 (3), pp.323–341.

58.     *'One American study'*: Livingston, G. (2019) 'The way U.S. teens spend their time is changing, but differences between boys and girls persist', *Pew Research Center*.

58.     *'we are experiencing another backlash'*: Kohn, A. (2006) *The homework myth: why our kids get too much of a bad thing.* Da Capo Books.

58.     *'primary schools are abandoning homework'*: see for example Boyd, M. (2018) 'Primary school bans homework because kids find it too "stressful"', *Daily Mirror*, 29 November.

58.     *Weekly homework hours are fewer in Finland, South Korea and Japan*: OECD (2014), *Does homework perpetuate inequities in education?*, PISA in Focus, No. 46, OECD Publishing.

58.     *Homework can lead to an extra five months' progress over one academic year*: Elliot Major, L. and Higgins, S. (2019) *What works? Research and evidence for successful teaching.* Bloomsbury.

59.   *'A good way to think about homework'*: Reilly, K. (2016) 'Is homework good for kids? Here's what the research says', *Time Magazine*, 30 August.

59.   *Effort is a stronger predictor of future academic grades*: Canadian Council on Learning (2009) *A systematic review of literature examining the impact of homework on academic achievement.*

## Other general references for this chapter

Cooper, H. (1989) *Homework*. Longman.

Cooper, H., Lindsay, J. L. and Nye, B. (2000) 'Homework in the home: how student, family, and parenting-style differences relate to the homework process', *Contemporary Educational Psychology*, 25 (4), pp.464–487.

Cooper, H., Robinson, J. C. and Patall, E. A. (2006) 'Does homework improve academic achievement? A synthesis of research, 1987–2003', *Review of Educational Research*, 76 (1), pp.1–62.

# 7. Arts and sports

**Did you know?**

The focus on English, maths and academic subjects in schools is squeezing out music, art and sport.

**Key takeaways**

- Arts and sports have huge educational value in themselves.
- They help to improve confidence, self-esteem and wellbeing, as well as social and leadership skills.
- Children should devote as much time to art and sport as scholarly study.

## More to life than academic grades

Their sad stories are the same: Oscar winners, renowned songwriters and singers, famous designers, best-selling authors, Olympic swimmers, and superstar footballers who have graced the sporting field. Many had a miserable time at school. Britain excels in the creative arts and sporting arenas. Yet its school system seems set up to crush the confidence of our creative, sporting and practical talents.

I meet thousands of teachers in my work. Most care deeply about the pupils they hope to nurture into fully formed adults prepared to prosper in life. And whenever I ask what their main worries are, one topic always rears its head. Their biggest fear is that the relentless focus on improving English, maths and 'core' academic subjects in our schools is squeezing out music, art and sport.

End-of-year high-stakes exams measure children solely on how well they can memorise facts and answer questions. That's fine if your dream is to one day immerse yourself in a life of academic study. But for so many other pupils these tests fail to recognise their different talents.[9] It can be completely disheartening.

It's just easier to produce marks for solving maths problems or summarising key points from written texts; it's much harder to measure creativity and communication, or quick thinking and leadership on the sports field. The problem for teachers is that their work is judged on how well their pupils do in these narrow tests. The results are made public in school league tables. Every extra minute is devoted to maximising these test scores; there is little time for anything else.

In primary schools, music, drama and physical education (PE) lessons are shelved to make way for extra sessions on reading and writing. Meanwhile, many secondary schools now start GCSE courses a year earlier. It's the only way to cover the huge amounts of material assessed in the exams. Hopes for a broader, more balanced curriculum are dashed again.

It's of little surprise that the numbers of children studying GCSEs in art and music have waned. Some argue the education system is producing factory-farmed children devoid of the wider skills deemed important by employers.

Subjects like art, music and sport have themselves been reduced to academic box-ticking exercises. It's not so much about the quality of your paintings or drawings, but how many technical terms you can fit into your written commentaries. At the start of university degree courses, lecturers will often tell students to forget everything they learned during their A-levels at school and start afresh again.

## Benefits

All this makes it even more important that parents know how much the arts and sports are central to human development. In my view, children should devote as much time to art and sport as scholarly study. They are sometimes called 'extracurricular activities'. This is a misnomer. They are as core to learning as maths or English.

What teachers instinctively believe is borne out by the research. Playing music, performing drama, producing a painting or sculpture, or playing a host of sports all have important educational value in themselves. They help to improve children's confidence. They are associated with increased self-esteem and wellbeing. They improve social and leadership skills.

---

9    It's tempting to quote words associated with Albert Einstein that 'if you judge a fish by its ability to climb a tree, it will live its whole life believing that it is stupid.' But it's unclear whether Einstein ever said these words. The Nobel Prize winning physicist however also had a poor time at school.

Learning to play an instrument is a valuable skill in itself, but has wider benefits as well, improving how children read and reason. Playing music or painting a picture strengthens a child's small muscles in their fingers, hands, and wrists – honing their fine motor skills. It makes learning to write much easier.

Regular exercise meanwhile has one obvious benefit. At a time when more and more children are becoming overweight, it can reduce the risk of being obese. Children also learn how to interact with other children when they play team sports. They develop an understanding of strategy and tactics. They learn how to cope with not winning.

Being involved in the arts is associated with more positive attitudes to learning. Children who learn to play an instrument, for example, also tend to do better at school. Similar benefits are reported from activities like drama and the fine arts, as well as digital design, photography and film-making.

Studies have suggested links between music and spatial awareness and between drama and writing. Choral singing has positive effects on wellbeing and emotional resilience. Some claim making music with other people reduces symptoms of depression, anxiety and loneliness.

A broader curriculum provides secondary benefits to children who are academic high achievers at school. They learn how to fail at something. This is important because otherwise they can arrive at university or the workplace unable to cope with suddenly finding out they can't do something.

There is increasing evidence that 'non-academic' skills are essential for getting on in life. Confidence, creativity and communication are increasingly valued by employers. As adults we are only too aware of what really matters in the workplace: how we interact with other people.

These personal skills will become even more important for jobs of the future as computers perform ever more number-crunching tasks (see chapter 20). The increasing numbers of young people armed with A grades at school and first-class degrees has put an extra premium on the other skills that distinguish candidates from the rest and all too often are not taught or nourished at many schools.

# What you can do

## Light the spark

More research is needed in this area. But what we do know mirrors much of the advice for academic learning. Your aim as a parent should be to light the creative or sporting spark in your children. Encourage and cajole them, and support them particularly when they are young. Praise their efforts.

Foster a spirit of trying new things. Only step in when it is really needed. If their heart is not in it, there is little point in forcing them to traipse around museums, achieve their piano grades, or swim 100 lengths. They must embrace it for themselves and eventually take the lead.

## Daily routines

Exercise or sport is best if it is regular. The NHS recommends that children should do at least 60 minutes of exercise every day. But research suggests benefits can be achieved through 30 minutes per day – particularly for children at high risk of being overweight.

Exercise should be of at least moderate intensity: this means working hard, but not too hard. If children are not exerting themselves at all, it's unlikely to have much impact. The more physical the activity, the greater the health benefits.

The same principle – a little a lot – applies to creative activities. If you're serious about learning a new instrument, then you need to do a short session every day rather than cramming it in before the tutor arrives. If you're not ready for the tutor, you won't be able to learn more from them. It's not a good use of the teaching session.

## Team benefits

Consider seeking out opportunities for your children to participate in groups, whether it is musical bands or team sports. They are great ways of learning how to work with other children or young people. Children can find the roles they are comfortable with in group dynamics.

## Check out coaches

Any activity is only as good as the coach or tutor that delivers it. How do you know they are good at what they do? What training and qualifications do they have? Most critically, is your child progressing with them? In the arts, the personal chemistry between teachers and learners can be key.

Educationalists argue that the best sports coaches are exemplars in how to provide direct and actionable feedback. They offer detailed steps of how to improve. School environments should mirror the sporting arena, instilling a belief in students that they can grow their talent and improve on their personal bests (see chapter 5).

Another example of model behaviour can be found in outdoor education programmes. These can set challenging goals, for example abseiling down a cliff face. Instructors provide continuous visual feedback and adjust their teaching. The learning goal is very clear to the teacher and students.

## Watch their diets

Taking part in sport doesn't necessarily mean that children will avoid being overweight. The research shows that children engaged in sporting activities eat more fruit and vegetables. But they also consume more fast food and sugary drinks. Healthy eating can boost self-esteem and sleep quality, and improve attention in the classroom. And it doesn't have to cost more.

## University clubs and societies

Finally, if your children go on to university, urge them to join clubs or societies. Leaving home for the first time to find yourself suddenly alone among thousands of other students can be an exciting but daunting experience. Taking a leap to join university societies or clubs is a quick way to make friends and learn new skills.

From debating to baking, wakeboarding to wine-making, polo, pool or politics, there will be something for everyone. Remember that university is as much a social as an academic experience. It will also show future employers that there's much more to your child than academic grades. The more they give, the more they will get back. Three years at university goes by very quickly.

### Five bits of advice

- Light the creative or sporting spark in your children, don't force it.
- Regular sessions get the best results.
- Group activities are great ways of learning how to work with others.
- Spend time assessing how good their coach or tutor is.
- Urge your children to join clubs or societies when they go to university.

# Reading and references

If I could recommend one thing to read it would be:

Elliot Major, L. and Higgins, S. (2019) *What works? Research and evidence for successful teaching*. Bloomsbury.

*What Works?* is an award-winning book for class teachers and school leaders which presents the research and evidence behind a range of school approaches and sets out practical steps for boosting the learning of pupils.

'Do we want a narrow but efficient range of subjects for all, or do we want to support a breadth of expertise and success across a wealth of subjects, which includes music, fine arts and drama?' write the authors. 'What would schooling look like if we valued English and mathematics for the value that they added to art and music achievement?'

## References

64.    *'What teachers instinctively believe is borne out by the research':* Elliot Major, L. and Higgins, S. (2019) *What works? Research and evidence for successful teaching*. Bloomsbury.

65.    *Children who learn instruments tend to do better at school/Studies have suggested links between music and spatial awareness and between drama and* writing: Elliot Major, L. and Higgins, S. (2019) *What works? Research and evidence for successful teaching*. Bloomsbury.

65.    *'Non-academic' skills are essential*: Heckman, J. and Mosso, S. (2014) 'The economics of human development and social mobility', *Annual Review of Economics*, 6 (1), pp.689–733.

66.    *Benefits are gained by exercising 30 minutes per day*: Elliot Major, L. and Higgins, S. (2019) *What works? Research and evidence for successful teaching*. Bloomsbury.

66.    *The best sports coaches are exemplars*: Wiliam, D. (2011) 'What is assessment for learning?', *Studies in Educational Evaluation*, 37, pp.3–14.

67.    *Children engaged in sporting activities eat more fruit and vegetables*: Elliot Major, L. and Higgins, S. (2019) *What works? Research and evidence for successful teaching*. Bloomsbury.

## Other general references for this chapter

Benz, S., Sellaro, R., Hommel, B. and Colzato, L. S. (2016) 'Music makes the world go round: the impact of musical training on non-musical cognitive functions – a review', *Frontiers in Psychology*, 6, 2023.

Catterall, J. S. (2012) *The arts and achievement in at-risk youth: findings from four longitudinal studies*. Research report #55. National Endowment for the Arts.

de Greeff, J. W., Bosker, R. J., Oosterlaan, J., Visscher, C. and Hartman, E. (2018) 'Effects of physical activity on executive functions, attention and academic performance in preadolescent children: a meta-analysis', *Journal of Science and Medicine in Sport*, 21 (5), pp.501–507.

Forgeard, M., Winner, E., Norton, A. and Schlaug, G. (2008) 'Practicing a musical instrument in childhood is associated with enhanced verbal ability and nonverbal reasoning', *PLOS One*, 3 (10), e3566.

OECD (2013) *Art for art's sake? The impact of arts education.*

Schucan-Bird, K., Tripney, J. and Newman, M. (2013) 'The educational impacts of young people's participation in organised sport: a systematic review', *Journal of Children's Services*, 8 (4), pp.264–275.

Secker, J., Spandler, H., Hacking, S., Kent, L. and Shenton, J. (2007) 'Art for mental health's sake', *Mental Health Today*, Jul–Aug, pp.34–36.

Singh, A., Uijtdewilligen, L., Twisk, J. W., Van Mechelen, W. and Chinapaw, M. J. (2012) 'Physical activity and performance at school: a systematic review of the literature including a methodological quality assessment', *Archives of Pediatrics & Adolescent Medicine*, 166 (1), pp.49–55.

Standley, J. M. (2008) 'Does music instruction help children learn to read? Evidence of a meta-analysis', *Update: Applications of Research in Music Education*, 27 (1), pp.17–32.

Trudeau, F. and Shephard, R. J. (2008) 'Physical education, school physical activity, school sports and academic performance', *International Journal of Behavioral Nutrition and Physical Activity*, 5 (1), 10.

# 8. Safeguarding summer-born children

**Key takeaways**
- Just because your children are the youngest in the class doesn't mean they are less talented than their older classmates!
- We should monitor summer-born children as we do other vulnerable groups.
- The priority is to boost self-esteem and confidence and to improve personal development.

## Summer-born disadvantage

Joe was never picked for the school council. He never made it onto the swimming team. He didn't win any school prizes. His school was ranked excellent by inspectors in every category. Yet his parents could never get away from the feeling that their son had been overlooked in class. They didn't want to make too much of a fuss though – they felt it would look like special pleading.

But there was always a nagging feeling that Joe was missing out. A few chosen pupils seemed to get all the adulation. They were relieved when Joe moved on to his next school.

I wish I could have told Joe's parents about the widely observed phenomenon of summer-born disadvantage. You see, Joe (like me) was born in August and so was one of the youngest in his class. That put him at a huge disadvantage – and not because he was any less talented than other pupils. It was just that he was less mature compared with his older classmates. Yet many teachers remain blissfully unaware of the systematic bias against summer-borns. This hidden disadvantage scars the lives of so many children.

It's of little surprise that older children perform better at school. In the Reception class at primary school, the eldest pupils have lived 25% longer than the youngest pupils. Autumn-born children are simply, on average, more cognitively, biologically and emotionally mature than their summer-born peers.

It is not that younger pupils have lower academic 'ability' or potential; it's just that they are less developed. The danger for younger pupils is that they end up with low self-esteem. We all tend to measure ourselves in relation to those around us. Low self-confidence creates a self-perpetuating problem. Pupils make less effort as they are scared of being seen as inferior. But in doing so they fall further behind their older peers, and are seen by teachers as struggling learners.

## Relative age effect

The 'relative age effect' is well documented in sport. Being bigger, stronger, faster and better-coordinated than average, older children are more likely to be selected for sports teams. This sets in train a self-fulfilling prophecy. They subsequently benefit from more support and coaching. They are helped to believe in themselves. They are more likely to develop into elite players. Younger children meanwhile suffer the crushing blow of rejection. They never get a second chance to show off their talents. They are forever left with a feeling of not being good enough.

The effect has been documented by England's Football Association. Over three times as many football players born between September and December make it into the academies of elite Premier League football clubs compared with those born between May and August. The report highlighted a shocking waste of talent: clubs miss out on thousands of summer-born footballers by failing to distinguish between physical maturity and true sporting ability.

The effect manifests itself at the very highest levels. I carried out my own investigation into the make-up of England's national football team at major tournaments over a 30-year period. This analysis was based on much smaller numbers of players: hundreds, not thousands. Yet the findings spoke for themselves: you are far less likely to play for England if you were born in June, July or August than if you were born in September, October or November. These startling facts can't be explained away by more people being born at different times of the year.[10]

## Education gaps

In education, the relative age effect has been confirmed by countless studies across the world. Being the youngest in the class has a big impact on a range of children's outcomes. Summer-born pupils are on average six months behind their older peers at age 7, three months behind at age 12, and still a month behind at age 16.

September-born students are 20% more likely to go to university than their August-born peers. Studies have suggested that someone born in October enjoys a 30% higher chance of securing a place at Oxbridge than someone born in July. In the academic race, when you are born matters.[11] These differences are life defining.

Summer-born pupils are more likely to have lower self-esteem and to be less confident in their own abilities. They are nearly twice as likely to suffer from behavioural difficulties. Many are misdiagnosed as having special educational needs by teachers who confuse immaturity with learning problems. If that wasn't enough, they are more likely to fall into risky behaviour such as underage smoking.

Hundreds of studies have documented the birthdate effect across the world. Success in school is influenced by date of birth across the entire curriculum in reading, writing, science and mathematics. Being just one month younger than a fellow pupil can mean poorer school results than your older peers.

## What you can do

### Ensure teachers are aware of the summer-born effect

Your first challenge, if you have a summer-born child, is to make sure that their teacher is aware of the summer-born effect.

It's hard to show what's happening in a single classroom or school. When it came to Joe, for example, the parents ummed and ahhed about whether to say something. They could see that there were other summer-born children in his class who were high achievers in the school. It felt as if they were trying to come up with an excuse.

---

10   If only the England football team followed the example of the all-conquering All Blacks rugby team, who ignore age when developing younger players. In education we call this the 'stage not age' approach.

11   The year of your birth matters for your life prospects as well. Those born and growing up in times of growing economies and opportunities do better in life than those growing up in times of recession.

What they failed to recognise was that those high achievers might have been even more successful had they been born a month or two later. Summer-born children are spread throughout the academic range. It is only when you look at the big picture over entire populations that the pattern emerges. Teachers need to be made aware of studies that have shown the summer-born effect is real for millions of pupils.

## Monitor as you would other vulnerable groups

Summer-borns should be treated as a vulnerable group in the same way that children with English as an additional language or those with special educational needs are. Keep an eye out for summer-borns indulging in risky behaviour or being diagnosed with special educational needs.

When discussing progress with teachers, talk about the maturity of your daughter or son. Particular attention should be paid to addressing low expectations and lack of confidence. Teachers will be well aware how these can stymie children's development. In education jargon, how is your teacher 'differentiating' the curriculum to cater for your child's needs?

## Call for age-adjusted selection and testing

A constant worry for summer-borns is being consigned to lower 'ability' sets or the second teams, delivering yet another blow to their sense of worth. Teachers should as a matter of routine consider younger as well as older children when appointing pupils into leadership roles at the school. It's also important to consider the impact on summer-born pupils when grouping children into sets or classes according to their academic achievement.

Pupils should be assessed in an age-adjusted way. This is easy to do: it means inflating scores for younger pupils so they are competing on a level playing field. Currently, some exams (such as tests to get into grammar schools) take age into account, while others inexplicably do not. I would challenge the results of any selection which does not take age into account.

These differences can be life defining if younger children miss out on the cut-off point to get into a particular class, or sixth form college or university. When you stop to think about this it makes no sense at all: are we really saying that younger pupils are less talented than older ones? Summer-born children are less likely to be selected for gifted and talented programmes. They are also more likely to take vocational rather than academic courses. We should be sympathetic to summer-born students who wish to re-sit their GCSE or A-level examinations.

Government ministers in England have allowed pupils to delay their school entry by a year so they become the oldest in the class. But this just creates a birthdate effect for other children. It means there will be others who are now the youngest in the class and less mature than their classmates.

The only way of tackling this inequity is to calculate age-adjusted scores in exams and tests, assessing a child's progress relative to others at their age, rather than older pupils in their class. Expected levels of progress should apply to a particular age rather than a particular point in time. Teachers should assess students in chronological age bands (by month of birth or season of birth) rather than as a whole class.

## Five bits of advice

- Ensure that your teachers are fully aware of the summer-born effect – it's extremely well documented across school systems.

- Try to avoid comparing your child with older peers in their class – think more about improving personal bests.

- Think of ways to boost self-esteem and confidence – these are so important for learning, as we will discuss elsewhere.

- Watch out for summer-borns being misdiagnosed with learning difficulties – teachers can mistake lack of maturity for other needs.

- Don't worry if your summer-born wants to take a year out or to re-sit their exams – it's probably quite natural given their relative age.

# Reading and references

If I could recommend one thing to read it would be:

Gladwell, M. (2009) *Outliers: the story of success.* Penguin.

Malcolm Gladwell's best-selling book challenges the idea that success in life is solely due to innate talent. It documents the relative age effect, showing for example how a disproportionate number of elite Canadian hockey players are born in the earlier months of the calendar year. Gladwell argues that arbitrary selection deadlines across society unfairly disadvantage younger talent: 'We need to replace the patchwork of lucky breaks and arbitrary advantages today that determine success – the fortunate birth dates and the happy accidents of history – with a society that provides opportunities for all.'

## References

71.    *Did you know?/'older children are more likely to be selected for sports teams'*: Cobley, S., Abraham, C. and Baker, J. (2008) 'Relative age effects on physical education attainment and school sport representation', *Physical Education and Sport Pedagogy*, 13 (3), pp.267–276.

     See also: Helsen, W. F., Baker, J., Schorer, J., Van Winckel, J. and Williams, M. A. (2013) 'The relative age effect in European professional soccer: is there any difference after ten years of research?', *Journal of Exercise, Movement, and Sport*, 45 (1).

72.    *'The effect has been documented by England's Football Association'*: Jackson, J. (2011) 'FA plans change for young talent to overcome the relative age effect', *The Observer*, 19 June.

73.    *'Summer-born pupils are on average six months behind their older peers at age 7, three months behind at age 12, and still a month behind at age 16'*: Elliot Major, L. and Higgins, S. (2019) *What works? Research and evidence for successful teaching.* Bloomsbury.

73.    *'September-born students are 20% more likely to go to university'*: Sykes, E. D. A., Bell, J. F. and Rodeiro, C. V. (2009) *Birthdate effects: a review of the literature from 1990-on.* Cambridge Assessment.

73.    *'someone born in October enjoys a 30% higher chance of securing a place at Oxbridge'*: Rosenbaum, M. (2013) 'Month of birth affects chance of attending Oxbridge', *BBC News*, 27 February.

73.    *'Summer-born pupils are more likely to have lower self-esteem'*: Crawford, C., Dearden, L. and Greaves, E. (2013) *When you are born matters: evidence for England.* IFS Reports (No. R80). Institute for Fiscal Studies.

74.   *Summer-born children are less likely to be selected for gifted and talented programmes/more likely to take vocational courses*: Elliot Major, L. and Higgins, S. (2019) *What works? Research and evidence for successful teaching.* Bloomsbury Education.

# 9. Private tutors

**Did you know?**

One-to-one tutoring can produce the greatest rate of progress for learners.

**Key takeaways**

- There is huge variation in the effectiveness of different tutors.
- Private tutoring is a completely unregulated market.
- How do you know tutoring is working for your child?

## Money well spent?

Private tutoring is education's Wild West. Many parents assume that all tutors are good at what they do. Otherwise they wouldn't be able to call themselves tutors, charge fees, or work for scholarly-sounding tutoring organisations competing in a billion-dollar global industry, right? Well, you couldn't be more wrong.

If there's one thing you should know about tutoring, it's this: there is huge variation in the effectiveness of tutors. For every tutor that might be an inspirational life-saver for your children, there's another who will make their life a misery. This is not just a matter of digging deep into your pockets. You need to ask whether you're getting your money's worth when you pay for extra tuition for your children. Alexander the Great's tutor was Aristotle; not everyone is so fortunate.

One-to-one tutoring is nonetheless one of education's best bets. The American educational psychologist Benjamin Bloom used it as the benchmark for the greatest rate of progress a learner can make. Studies suggest that when delivered well in schools, face-to-face tutoring can lead to an extra five months' learning gain for pupils during one academic year. But remember, this is only an average result produced under ideal conditions in school environments. Even trials of gold standard tutoring programmes, packed with detailed guidance, undertaken by trained teachers, have produced mixed results.

For any approach, delivery is key. One of the most important ideas in education is the Bananarama principle, named after Bananarama and Fun Boy Three's 1982 hit single 'It Ain't What You Do'.[12] The principle states that it's not what you do but the way you do it that counts. It's a point that is so often overlooked in education as well as in life. It's particularly true for tutoring.

Few global industries have grown at such rapid pace over recent decades. This has been driven by the insatiable demand of anxious parents. The tutoring sector is now valued at hundreds of billions of dollars across the world. According to the Sutton Trust, a quarter of pupils aged 11 to 16 in the UK have received private tuition. The UK still has some way to go to catch up with South Korea, where spending by households on private tutoring now rivals government education budgets.

But this is a completely unregulated market. Many tutors lack training or qualifications. Tutors can be students, graduates, teachers, teaching assistants or retired educators. For many, tutoring remains a part-time job, while they look for something else. A select few super-tutors may be paid hundreds of pounds an hour, teaching the offspring of privileged elites. But the average hourly rate for the thousands of rank-and-file tutors in the UK is more like £30 an hour. Tutoring organisations range from large corporate players to charities to social enterprises to sole traders.

Tutoring is a good investment, but paying for it needs thought and careful planning. How do you know it is working for your child?

---

12   This principle was coined by my friend and academic collaborator, Steve Higgins, when we first toured the country giving talks to teachers about the best bets for classroom practice. We used the principle to explain the variation in outcomes for children from different approaches when we launched the Pupil Premium Toolkit. Published by the Sutton Trust charity in 2011, the toolkit offered an accessible Which?-style guide detailing best bets for improving children's attainment.

# What you can do

## What is your tutor's background?

Have tutors been teachers? One-to-one tutoring is a very different skill to whole-class teaching, but school tutoring programmes involving trained teachers have twice the effect of those deploying teaching assistants or volunteers. Four in ten state school teachers have tutored outside normal working hours.

This is not to say you shouldn't consider other tutors. But if you use students or graduates then there they are just a riskier bet. You need to ask more questions. Have they received any training? Do they have the appropriate safeguarding requirements? Do they have relevant experience or positive reviews from other clients? Students and graduates can still be highly effective, and a cheaper option. One study found children who received tutoring from trained university undergraduates did better in maths at primary school. But knowing a subject well does not necessarily equate to being able to teach.

Julia Silver, a senior leader in a primary school in London and an experienced tutor, told me that parents should consider whether tutors are qualified to teach their child, in this subject, today. 'I think of it like shoes – you need the right shoes for the exact age and stage and purpose,' she said. 'And in the same way that you wouldn't let your child wear shoes that are a bad fit, you shouldn't stick with tutors that aren't a good fit. How do you tell? You watch your child. Not for enthusiasm (dream on) but for a sense of 'this helps'. Tutors are supposed to help.'

## Check them out

The most reliable way of finding out whether a tutor is right for your child is to try them out. Trial and error is the most effective approach I've seen, whether the tutor's helping with playing the piano, learning to swim, practising a foreign language, brushing up on maths, or prepping for exams. It's very hard to predict on paper how good a teacher will be, and also what the personal chemistry will be with their tutee. Be aware that the same tutor might work well with one child, but not their brother or sister.

## A little a lot

The best results follow the universal educational law: a little a lot spread over time. In schools, one-to-one or small-group tutoring may be organised in daily sessions of 30 minutes over a school term. Sessions at home with private tutors can be weekly, but also daily when preparing for imminent examinations.

The best tutoring links with what is being covered in the classroom. It should complement school teaching, not contradict it. It's best to inform your classroom teacher if your child is receiving private tutoring.

## Set clear targets

Set clear targets with deadlines. If you don't see progress after a month, you should review the situation. Don't be afraid to change the tutor, or the approach. Make sure you schedule regular updates with tutors to assess progress.

Many studies have shown face-to-face tuition works; we have far less evidence of the impact of online tutoring. If sessions are done over the internet, then you should review how successful they have been. It may be that a blended approach is best, combining face-to-face and online sessions. Studies have found that tuition in groups of two or three pupils is as effective as one-to-one tuition. Is this worth considering?

## Avoid creating dependent learners

Remember, the goal of all good teaching is to create independent learners. You will need to watch out that extra tutoring doesn't lead to a dependency mindset in which your child always needs help to do their work. The hope is to boost children's confidence rather than undermine it. Being given extra support can make them feel they are failing or not good enough.

Many parents feel pressured to pay for tutoring because they know other parents are doing the same. Before you commit to tutoring, ask yourself: Why do you think extra tutoring is required? Is this a joint decision with your children? Have you sought out advice from classroom teachers?

## Does your tutor believe?

If tutors are convinced their tutees are capable of making progress then they are more likely to do so. Do they believe in a growth mindset? This inner belief is a characteristic of effective teachers.

## Ask teachers about tutoring in schools

If you can't afford to pay for a tutor, there may be other options available. You can ask what tutoring is available in school for your children, with so many government- and charity-supported tutoring programmes now available. Ask teachers why they are adopting a particular approach. Is this small-group tutoring or one-to-one? How many sessions are planned? How are tutors being trained? What are the expected gains?

## Five bits of advice

- If your tutor is not a trained teacher, do your homework: do they have the credentials to be a good bet?
- The best way to assess whether a tutor will work for your child is to try them out.
- Mention tutoring to your classroom teacher – they may be able to offer some advice on what to tutor on.
- Online tutoring is less proven than face-to-face sessions, but you might consider a mix of the two.
- Watch out for a dependency mindset.

# Reading and references

If I could recommend one thing to read it would be:

Slavin. R. (2020) 'The details matter. That's why proven tutoring programs work better than general guidelines.' Robert Slavin's blog.

I enjoyed many discussions with the late American psychologist Robert Slavin, who was one of the world's experts on tutoring. In one of his last blogs, Slavin argued that tutoring has to have several crucial features to be effective. These include feedback and correction strategies when pupils make errors, ways of motivating pupils, and links between tutors and teachers and between tutors and parents.

'Tutoring derives its unique effectiveness from the ability of the tutor to personalize instruction for each child,' he wrote. 'It also depends on close relationships between tutors and students.'

## References

79. *Did you know?*: Bloom, B. S. (1984) 'The 2 sigma problem: the search for methods of group instruction as effective as one-to-one tutoring', *Educational Researcher*, 13 (6), pp.4–16.

80. *'face-to-face tutoring can lead to an extra five months learning gain'*: Higgins, S., Katsipataki, M., Coleman, R., Henderson, P., Major, L. E., Coe, R. and Mason, D. (2015) *The Sutton Trust–Education Endowment Foundation teaching and learning toolkit*. Education Endowment Foundation.

80. *Trials of gold standard tutoring programmes have produced mixed results*: Baye, A., Inns, A., Lake, C. and Slavin, R. E. (2019) 'A synthesis of quantitative research on reading programs for secondary students', *Reading Research Quarterly*, 54 (2), pp.133–166.

80. *'a quarter of pupils aged 11 to 16 in the UK have received private tuition'*: Kirby, P. (2016) *Shadow schooling: private tuition and social mobility in the UK*. The Sutton Trust.

80. *Spending on private tutoring in South Korea rivals government education budgets*: Bray, M. (2009) *Confronting the shadow education system: what government policies for what private tutoring?* UNESCO.

81. *'school tutoring programmes involving trained teachers have twice the effect'*: Elliot Major, L. and Higgins, S. (2019) *What works? Research and evidence for successful teaching*. Bloomsbury.

81.   *'children who received tutoring from trained university undergraduates did better in maths'*: Torgerson, C., Bell, K., Coleman, E., Elliott, L., Fairhurst, C., Gascoine, L., Hewitt, C. and Torgerson, D. (2018) *Tutor trust: affordable primary tuition.* Education Endowment Foundation.

82.   *tuition in groups of two or three pupils is as effective as one-to-one tuition'*: Elliot Major, L. and Higgins S. (2019) *What works? Research and evidence for successful teaching.* Bloomsbury.

## Other general references for this chapter

Cooper, H., Nye, B., Charlton, K., Lindsay, J. and Greathouse, S. (1996) 'The effects of summer vacation on achievement test scores: a narrative and meta-analytic review', *Review of Educational Research*, 66 (3), pp.227–268.

Clay, M. M. (2007) *Literacy lessons designed for individuals part one: Why? When? and How?* Heinemann.

Cohen, P. A., Kulik, J. A. and Kulik, C. C. (1982) 'Education outcomes of tutoring: a meta-analysis of findings', *American Educational Research Journal*, 19, pp.237–248.

Dang, H-A. and Halsey Rogers, F. (2008) 'The growing phenomenon of private tutoring: does it deepen human capital, widen inequalities, or waste resources?' *The World Bank Research Observer*, 23 (2), pp.161–2000.

D'Agostino, J. V. and Harmey, S. J. (2016) 'An international meta-analysis of reading recovery', *Journal of Education for Students Placed at Risk (JESPAR)*, 21 (1), pp.29–46.

Drabble, C. (2016) *Bloomsbury CPD library: supporting children with special educational needs and disabilities.* Bloomsbury.

Elliot Major, L. and Machin, S. (2018) *Social mobility and its enemies.* Penguin.

Pellegrini, M., Lake, C., Inns, A. and Slavin, R. E. (2018) 'Effective programs in elementary mathematics: a best-evidence synthesis', *Best Evidence Encyclopedia*.

Slavin, R. E., Lake, C., Davis, S. and Madden, N. A. (2011) 'Effective programs for struggling readers: a best-evidence synthesis', *Educational Research Review*, 6 (1), pp.1–26.

Tanner, E., Day, N., Tennant, R., Turczuk, O., Ireson, J., Rushforth, K. and Smith, K. (2009) *Private tuition in England.* Department for Children, Schools and Families.

# 10. Revision strategies: thinking hard or thinking lazy?

> **Did you know?**
> Revision strategies that focus on testing our knowledge are far more effective than popular approaches such as highlighting and re-reading.

> **Key takeaways**
> - Learning happens when people have to think hard.
> - Taking a quiz or test is one of the most effective learning approaches we know.
> - Revising a little a lot over time is much more effective than doing a lot at one time.

## How to remember things

Do they make children think hard or think lazy? This is the question we should ask ourselves to find out which approaches are the best ways to remember things. So much of what children do when they are trying to lodge facts and figures into their minds is ineffectual. Most revision involves shallow thinking.

There is no easy way around this. We need to work our brains to embed things in our long-term memories. When it comes to mental exertion, it's exactly the same as physical effort: no pain, no gain (and when you have done it once, do it again).

Surface-level skimming of material just doesn't cut it. Hours slumped over desks lazily looking over books is frankly a waste of time. You would be much better off trying short bursts of intense work and taking breaks in between. In education, quality always trumps quantity.

It is why the amount of effort children make doing their homework, measured by questions attempted, is a much stronger predictor of future academic grades than the amount of time they spend on homework (see chapter 6).

Education and assessment expert Rob Coe says that 'learning happens when people have to think hard'. Psychologist Daniel Willingham says that 'memory is the residue of thought'. The more you think about something, the more likely you'll remember it. We don't remember all our fleeting thoughts, only those that we pay most attention to.

In classrooms we are fooled into thinking learning is going on just because there is a buzz of noise and activity. We use these signals because that's all we can see. The truth is that learning is probably the last thing on pupils' minds!

In his best-selling book *Thinking, Fast and Slow*, Nobel prize winner Daniel Kahneman explains how our brains are hardwired to conserve energy. We are born to think fast, making quick snap judgements; it takes huge effort to think slow, studying things more deeply. In other words, it's completely natural for our children to be lazy. We have just evolved that way.

To make matters worse, trainee teachers aren't routinely taught what approaches work best for memorising things. Studies show that many of the revision techniques children like to use aren't good for learning, while many of the things they avoid – you've guessed it – are the best ways to memorise information.

All this is important to know: it can make all the difference in your children's progress, and improve their grades in end-of-year exams. Children need to think actively about information to remember it. Simply being repeatedly exposed to information won't work. You need to ask: does this revision approach encourage hard or lazy thinking?

## Limits of highlighting, re-reading and summarising

Most notes and exercise books are covered with the bright colours of highlighter pens. Children love highlighting texts to identify key words, equations and phrases. It gives them a sense of being on top of the material without having to do much work. Little thought is required.

But unfortunately it isn't a good technique for revising. One problem is that highlighting is done poorly: pupils fail to pick out the main points they need to learn. Another is that merely highlighting or underlining text doesn't transfer the words into your long-term memory (see chapter 12).

Re-reading and summarising texts are also among the most popular revision strategies. But there is very little evidence yet available which demonstrates that studying material again after an initial reading is as useful as other approaches such as practice tests. Summarising a page of text into a few short lines and note taking have been found to be little better. But as with highlighting, one problem is that pupils often produce poor summaries, failing to flesh out the main points of a text or including incorrect information.

## Test yourself

It seems obvious to say that you don't really know you know something until you test yourself. But our brains are programmed to preserve energy. That's why our children will do anything to avoid tests.

But testing yourself forces you to try to generate answers. Retrieving previously learned things creates stronger memories. Testing has been shown to help children of all ages and capabilities. It works for all types of exams.

What in education is termed as 'retrieval practice' can be done in many ways: practice tests, previous exam papers, multiple choice tests, tests made up of questions you've set yourself. Tests reveal the things you need to read up on. Your children can also list questions in notes as they learn material. These can be 'why' questions as well as 'what' questions. Simply explaining something to themselves helps too.

No-one else can generate a memory for your child. It's down to them. The psychologists Elizabeth Bjork and Robert Bjork sum it up best: 'Basically, any time that you, as a learner, look up an answer or have somebody tell or show you something that you could, drawing on current cues and your past knowledge, generate instead, you rob yourself of a powerful learning opportunity.'

## A little a lot, not a lot at once

Many of us are prone to last-minute cramming before examinations. I learned the hard way about the downfalls of this approach. After revising through the night for my first university exam, I woke up to find to my horror that I was still in bed when the exam was halfway through. I've been a stickler for being on time ever since.

Revising a little a lot over time is a much more effective approach than doing a lot at one time. In education this is called spacing. It is effective because it allows children time to forget information and re-learn it. This cements the material in their long-term memory. Unlike the crammer, the spacer remembers the material long after the exam.

This is why it's good to heed a teacher's advice and produce a revision plan setting out what your child will do over a number of weeks. Leave at least a day between different topics or subjects. Combine this approach with lots of self-tests.

And remember the rule of three. In his research on what children really do in classrooms, Graham Nuttall found that pupils need to encounter information three times to learn it properly (see chapter 15). This suggests your children should try to test themselves three separate times for something to stick.

## Alternate between types of questions and topics

A promising revision strategy is to mix topics or questions at the same time, rather than focusing on one kind of question. In education this is called interleaving. This technique has long been known to be a powerful enhancer of learning. And yet to this day it is ignored in many textbooks.

Interleaving is a particularly useful tool in mathematics. Textbooks introducing basic maths, for example, will group questions by different topics – addition problems, then subtraction problems, followed by multiplication problems. Pupils will learn more effectively if they mix the questions up, combining addition and multiplication problems, for example. Children have to think harder about the strategies they are using when they switch between problems.

One note of caution: alternating topics works within subjects. But switching between completely different subjects – say maths and history – may just lead to confusion. If a subject is completely new, your child may need to go through it all first, before switching.

## Mnemonics

There are many strategies for improving memorisation (these are known as 'metamemory' techniques). Memory can be improved using short-term tricks such as acronyms, rhymes, mnemonics or repetition. Long-term strategies include playing memory games or building a 'mind palace'. In your mind, you walk through different rooms with images related to things you want to remember. Mind palaces don't work for everyone.

Mnemonics are clever short-cuts to memorising. They work by using memorable acronyms to spell out terms or by associating words with other things to aid memory. Every generation tries to come up with more memorable acronyms.

Growing up, I used 'Roy G Biv' to remember the colours of the rainbow: red, orange, yellow, green, blue, indigo, violet. My son used 'I Peed Myself At Tesco Carpark' to remember the stages of the cell cycle: interphase, prophase, metaphase, anaphase, telophase and cytokinesis. It's more fun and probably more effective to come up with your own versions.

Mnemonics are useful for memorising topics for talks or remembering names or key facts. But they can be more useful as a quick fix rather than a tool for long-term learning.

## Final comments

In summary, an ideal revision approach would include lots of testing, spaced over time, switching between topics. There is no harm in highlighting or summarising texts. But too much time spent on these approaches means less time on more effective strategies.

One final point: many teenagers like to watch videos or listen to music while revising. Given everything we know about how our minds work, this is likely to be a damaging distraction. If possible it would be better to do short bouts of revision with entertainment in between. But some children swear they can retain information while listening to music, and if that's the only way you can get them to revise, go with it!

### Five bits of advice

- Does the revision approach encourage hard or lazy thinking?
- Highlighting, re-reading and summarising texts has little impact on memorising material.
- Testing what you know through quizzes or tests is the best revision strategy we have.
- Follow a revision plan to space learning over a number of weeks, leaving at least a day before coming back to the same topic or subject.
- Mnemonics are useful for memorising vocabulary and basic facts.

# Reading and references

If I could recommend one thing to read it would be:

Pashler, H., Bain, P., Bottge, B., Graesser, A., Koedinger, K., McDaniel, M. and Metcalfe, J. (2007) *Organizing instruction and study to improve student learning*. National Center for Education Research, Institute of Education Sciences, US Department of Education.

This is a useful expert guide offering seven practical strategies to help students master new knowledge and skills – and to not forget what they have learned. The approaches are developed from a careful reading of the latest research on learning and memory. The authors argue that 'learning depends upon memory, and that memory of skills and concepts can be strengthened by relatively concrete and in some cases quite non-obvious strategies.'

## References

87.  *Did you know?*: Coe, R., Aloisi, C., Higgins, S. and Elliot Major, L. (2014) *What makes great teaching?* The Sutton Trust.

88.  *'learning happens when people have to think hard'*: Coe, R. (2013) 'Improving education: a triumph of hope over experience'. Inaugural lecture, Durham University.

88.  *'memory is the residue of thought'*: Willingham, D. T. (2008) 'What will improve a student's memory?' *American Educator*, 32 (4), pp.17–25.

88.  *'Daniel Kahneman explains how our brains are hardwired to conserve energy'*: Kahneman, D. (2011) *Thinking, fast and slow*. Farrar, Straus and Giroux.

88.  *Highlighting isn't a good technique for revising*: Dunlosky, J., Rawson, K. A., Marsh, E. J., Nathan, M. J. and Willingham, D. T. (2013) 'Improving students' learning with effective learning techniques: promising directions from cognitive and educational psychology', *Psychological Science in the Public Interest*, 14 (1), pp.4–58.

89.  *Testing helps children of all ages and capabilities*: Dunlosky, J., Rawson, K. A., Marsh, E. J., Nathan, M. J. and Willingham, D. T. (2013) 'Improving students' learning with effective learning techniques: promising directions from cognitive and educational psychology', *Psychological Science in the Public Interest*, 14 (1), pp.4–58.

     See also: Rosenshine, B., Meister, C. and Chapman, S. (1996) 'Teaching students to generate questions: a review of the intervention studies', *Review of Educational Research*, 66 (2), pp.181–221.

89.   *'Basically, any time that you, as a learner, look up an answer'*: Bjork, E. and Bjork, R. (2011) 'Making things hard on yourself, but in a good way: creating desirable difficulties to enhance learning', in Gernsbacher, M. A., Pew, R. W., Hough, L. M. and Pomerantz, J. R. (eds.) *Psychology and the real world: essays illustrating fundamental contributions to society*, pp.56–64. Worth Publishers.

89.   *Spacing is effective*: Sobel, H. S., Cepeda, N. J. and Kapler, I. V. (2011) 'Spacing effects in real-world classroom vocabulary learning', *Applied Cognitive Psychology*, 25 (5), pp.763–767.

90.   *Interleaving is a powerful enhancer of learning*: Rohrer, D., Dedrick, R. F. and Stershic, S. (2015) 'Interleaved practice improves mathematics learning', *Journal of Educational Psychology*, 107 (3), pp.900–908.

90.   *'Mnemonics are clever short-cuts to memorising'*: Willingham, D. T. (2008) 'What will improve a student's memory?' *American Educator*, 32 (4), pp.17–25.

See also: Peters, E. E. and Levin, J. R. (1986) 'Effects of a mnemonic imagery strategy on good and poor readers' prose recall', *Reading Research Quarterly*, 21 (2), pp.179–192.

# 11. Helicopter awareness of learning

**Did you know?**

Helicopter learning or 'metacognitive' strategies are among the most powerful ways of boosting learning skills.

**Key takeaways**

- Helicopter learning can be learned, providing skills to prosper at school and in life.
- Strategies to plan, do and review help children to become independent learners.
- There are many ways to create a more 'can do' attitude to problem-solving.

## Helicopter learning

It was as if a learning fog had descended on Jack, making it impossible for him to plan ahead. For years our son struggled with writing essays or answering questions requiring long written answers. He would be unsure of how to start, let alone how he might finish. Like so many children he would just launch into the writing, only to grind to a shuddering halt before the first paragraph was complete.

He found it incredibly demoralising, and began to believe he just wasn't good enough to do extended pieces of writing.[13] After many long hours trying to help Jack, we came up with a trick that seemed to open up his eyes to the possibility of what he could achieve. This was to imagine piloting a helicopter: to rise up from the quagmire below and gain a bird's-eye view of the learning landscape stretching ahead. During this imaginary flight we would run through the following check-list of questions.

## Planning

- Where are we trying to get to? (i.e. what are your learning goals?)
- What did I find out last time we did something similar?
- What's the best way of planning for the journey ahead? (I.e. what learning strategies are you planning to use?)
- Where did I get stuck last time?

## Doing

- Am I on the right track?
- Am I on time?
- Do I need to slow down or speed up?

## Reviewing

- Did what I do work? (I.e. were the strategies used effective?)
- What could I have done better?
- What tips have I learned for next time?

Experienced learners go through these three stages – planning, monitoring and reviewing – when they do any piece of work.[14] If Jack needed prompting, I would think out aloud, explaining how I would wrestle with these questions.

We would discuss simple techniques such as writing out a plan for the essay, splitting it up into bite-sized chunks. We would sketch out a plan for the beginning and ending. For more creative tasks we might draw a mind-map sprawled over a large piece of paper to link ideas in a non-linear way. I would be careful not to throw too much in. The aim was for Jack to be in the driving seat. It took time, but little by little we found it lifted Jack's learning to new levels.

---

13    Jack was later diagnosed with attention deficit hyperactivity disorder (ADHD), which explained why he struggled to concentrate and organise his thoughts.

14    Plan, do and review is also a technique British athletes used to great success in the 2012 Olympic games.

## Metacognition and self-regulation

This exercise was our version of what educators call 'metacognition and self-regulation' strategies. They aim to improve pupils' thinking about the way they learn. When I first spoke to teachers about these scientific-sounding terms I remember their blank faces. Meta is the Greek term meaning 'on top of'; metacognition simply means 'on top of thinking'.[15] Self-regulation meanwhile describes how we manage our thoughts and emotions.

It is one of the most powerful ways we know of improving learning. Some educators have called it a magical tool, an approach with educational superpowers. It can lead to the holy grail of teaching: getting pupils to become independent learners, totally in charge of their own helicopters.

Yet it's a topic that is bedevilled by jargon. Millions of articles have been written about metacognition and self-regulation. But most don't practise what they preach. They read more like abstract scientific journal articles than accessible guides for teachers. To make matters worse, the experts disagree on what things are covered by the 'metacognition and self-regulation' banner. But this is a topic that's worth paying attention to because it's so important.

The power of helicopter learning is its ability to turn bad learning habits into good ones. That's a life-transforming skill. Many children fall into the trap of believing they are just not good enough to be high achievers, no matter how much they try. But the miracle of metacognition is that its tricks and techniques can be learned. These skills are good for prospering in school but in life as well.

## What you can do

### Help to create a 'can do' attitude

Whenever our son used to give up on a task and say 'I'm just not clever enough' it would feel like a stab to the heart. No parent wants to see their children being despondent when faced with an exercise set by their teacher. Jack would put off doing schoolwork until the very last minute. Producing an extended piece of writing or completing pages of maths questions seemed like an impossible challenge. As battle-hardened adults we know that in life there are much bigger obstacles to come. Having a negative mindset isn't going to help.

There are many ways that parents can help to create a more 'can do' attitude to problem-solving. One of the tricks of good teaching is to sneak in new ideas

---

15   The Greek philosopher Aristotle among others wrote about the importance of thinking about thinking.

without the learners knowing it. Metaphors can be powerful: imagining piloting a helicopter allows you to rise above a problem so it's more doable; a more down to earth option is to picture a car 'driving' your brain.

Another trick is to think aloud: reveal the internal conversations you have in your own head when you approach a problem. It's important to show how you as a parent have struggled too, and have made mistakes, but have found ways of getting round difficult obstacles. What strategies have you used?

But be careful not to overload your child with too much too quickly. They can only take on so much. At the same time, they need to be challenged in order to make the learning interesting. It's easy to miss this sweet spot. Too hard and pupils will not be able to think metacognitively; too easy and they won't need to. Be specific. Introducing these techniques works best when done with concrete school tasks rather than explaining them in abstract terms.

## Reducing anxiety

Remember that how we think and how we feel are inseparable for learners. If we're feeling anxious, we're less likely to be strategic or reflective. Strategies that may help reduce these feelings could be as simple as taking short breaks during an assignment. One approach I've tried with students is the breathing exercises actors use to calm themselves down before performances. This could be just taking ten deep breaths, focusing on inhaling in and out in equal measure. Many meditation practices can also help.

Teaching these techniques can help children navigate life situations that will come their way thick and fast as they grow up. Asking children to think about their behaviour can be a more productive approach than just confronting or criticising them. Self-regulated learners are aware of their strengths and weaknesses. They are more likely to overcome risk aversion, failure, distractions, and laziness in the pursuit of a goal.

## Reflect on parenting styles

You can also reflect on whether your parenting style promotes metacognition and self-regulation. Helicopter learning is the opposite of helicopter parenting. Following your child's every move will not help them develop their thinking skills. Being overly authoritarian – 'do as I say, not as I do' – won't help either. Children need to be allowed to reflect on their own decisions, and develop their own set of problem-solving skills.

Having over-involved parents appears to lead to a host of bad life outcomes, including higher levels of depression and stress, less satisfaction with life, less confidence in your abilities, and poor relationships with your peers.

## Talk to your teachers

If you suspect that something else is to blame for why your child struggles with metacognition, talk to their teacher about the possibility of your child having a learning disability. If that's the case, the school can arrange an evaluation and help get the tools needed to boost problem-solving skills. So many parents regret not getting their children diagnosed earlier. Don't put this off!

## Five bits of advice

- Talk about the power of helicopter learning strategies and how these can be learned.
- Reveal your own internal dialogue when trying to overcome problems.
- Consider strategies that can reduce anxiety.
- Is your parenting style hindering or helping helicopter learning?
- Talk to your teachers if you think your child might have a learning disability.

# Reading and references

If I could recommend one thing to read it would be:

Nilson, L. B. (2013) Creating Self-Regulated Learners: strategies to strengthen students' self-awareness and learning skills. Stylus Publishing.

Linda Nilson's book is underpinned by the conviction that all children are capable of becoming self-regulated learners, and that self-regulation is a fundamental prerequisite of academic success. Nilson presents an array of tested activities and assignments through which students can progressively reflect on, monitor and improve their learning skills. 'Study skills really aren't the point,' writes Nilson. 'Learning is about one's relationship with oneself and one's ability to exert the effort, self-control, and critical self-assessment necessary to achieve the best possible results – and about overcoming risk aversion, failure, distractions, and sheer laziness in pursuit of REAL achievement. This is self-regulated learning.'

## References

98.    *'Self-regulated learners are more likely to overcome risk aversion, failure, distractions, and laziness'*: Elliot Major, L. and Higgins, S. (2019) *What works? Research and evidence for successful teaching.* Bloomsbury.

99.    *Over-involved parents lead to a host of bad life outcomes*: Dewar, G. (2018) *Parenting styles: an evidence-based, cross-cultural guide.*

## Other general references for this chapter

Dignath, C., Buettner, G. and Langfeldt, H. (2008) 'How can primary school students learn self-regulated learning strategies most effectively? A meta-analysis on self-regulation training programmes', *Educational Research Review*, 3 (2), pp.101–129.

Fogarty, R. and Pete, B. (2018) *Metacognition: the neglected skill set for empowering students.* Hawker Brownlow Education.

Higgins, S., Hall, E., Baumield, V. and Moseley, D. (2005) *A meta-analysis of the impact of the implementation of thinking skills approaches on pupils.* Research Evidence in Education Library. EPPI Centre, Social Science Research Unit, Institute of Education, University of London.

Quigley, A., Muijs, D. and Stringer, E. (2018) *Metacognition and self-regulated learning: guidance report.* Education Endowment Foundation.

The Global Metacognition Institute (website).

Zimmerman, B. J. (1990) 'Self-regulated learning and academic achievement: an overview', *Educational Psychologist*, 25 (1), pp.3–17.

# 12. Mind matters: managing cognitive load

**Did you know?**

We can only retain a few chunks of new information in our working memory.

**Key takeaway**

- Cognitive load theory is a theory of how our brain works. Avoid overloading your children's working memories with too much information so they are freed up to learn.

## Cognitive load theory

If there is one part of our bodies riddled with myths and misconceptions, it is our magical learning machine: the brain. I always remember one of the toughest boys in my class at school arguing that the people with the biggest brains would obviously become neurosurgeons. I could see his logic, but I knew it didn't quite work like that. I just didn't want to pick a fight.

We've all been seduced by myths about the brain during our lives. We only use 10% of our brains, right? Well, no, we use a lot more. Surely it's true that we are either right-brained or left-brained? Well, actually, we all use both sides of our brains. Don't our minds develop at a steady pace as we grow up? It sounds very plausible. But they don't. Our mental capacity develops in fits and starts.

This last point is an important one for parents. Many anxious mums and dads have come to me for advice over the years, concerned that their children have got stuck at school. Sometimes parents have to stand back and remember that learning is a long and winding road with many ups and downs, not a linear track.

The good parent educator needs to know the difference between genuine cognitive science insights and neuro-myths. And one of the most powerful ideas to emerge is cognitive load theory (CLT). This is a theory of how our brain works. The key idea is this: what we know is stored in our limitless long-term memory, but any new information we take in has to first pass through our limited working memory. The best way to start you off on this theory is to do a simple exercise.

First, a question: how many chunks of information can your children hold in their short-term memory at any one given time?

    A. One

    B. Four

    C. Seven

    D. Ten

    E. Twenty

Now you can find out for yourselves. Ask your children to remember five words. Then take their attention away by focusing them on something else, perhaps asking a few simple questions. Ask them to list the five words again. How many do they still remember?

Our brains have an amazing capacity for remembering things. But according to cognitive load theory there is one snag: the gateway to our long-term memory gets clogged up very quickly. We can only retain a few chunks of new information in our working memory at any one time. It was once thought this magic number was seven. Now experts believe it is four or five. So the correct answer to the above question for most people is either B or C.

Cognitive load theory is very popular among teachers as it confirms what they have always instinctively known is good teaching practice. Learners need just enough new information to add to what they already know. Too much, and our working memory gets overloaded. No new information can get through.

Our capacity for learning is related to what we know. Knowledge gives us cognitive power. What we have already embedded in our long-term memory frees up our working memory to take on new ideas and facts. We learn things when we are able to think about them properly and retrieve them from our long-term memory.

But remember that cognitive load theory is just an idea. It is hard to prove or disprove scientifically. There is no actual physical location in the brain that houses short-term memory. But the theory is helpful for parents because it highlights good learning practices.

# What you can do

## Break it down

If your child is struggling with a problem, it may be because their working memory is being overloaded with too much new information. Break the problem down into smaller chunks. Pause regularly. Can they learn these components first before bringing them together to solve the whole problem?

Remember to get the balance right: too much new information blocks up working memory. Too little means no learning takes place. If we want to remember something, we have to think about it.

## Go through a worked example

Show your children how to solve a problem with a worked example. This involves providing the answer to the problem up front, accompanied by the working out needed to solve it. It's a step-by-step guide to answering the problem. Then gradually remove your help and answers until they can do the problems on their own.

Cognitive load theory provides reassuring evidence for teachers who use explicit instruction in the classroom. This is where they show pupils what to do and how to do it, rather than having them discover information for themselves.

## Show and tell

Present new information in pictures as well as spoken words. Our working memories have two separate channels – one for visual information, the other for auditory information. Spreading the load creates more cognitive space.

But avoid reading out text aloud while children are reading it. Adding verbal explanation to written words is just adding extra cognitive load that will clog up working memory.

Encourage your children to visualise what they have learned in images: it helps them to better understand and recall information. Generating an image while reading requires a reader to be actively engaged with the text. You can share the image you've created in your mind, and talk about which words inspired your picture.

## Kim's game

Try Kim's game.[16] Put letters, pictures, or words on a tray, show them to your child, and then cover them up and ask them to name the objects. Alternatively, you can remove the items and get them to guess what has been removed. The game develops a person's capacity to observe and remember details.

## No TV

Listening to music or watching videos while doing schoolwork is not recommended! Studies have found that prolonged TV viewing may actually diminish our short-term memory capacity, damaging development in reading, maths and language development.

### Five bits of advice

- Cognitive load theory suggests we should focus on good teaching practice: don't overload children with too much information.
- Break problems down into smaller chunks.
- Use worked examples to approach problems and gradually take away support for children.
- Present new information in pictures and spoken words.
- Avoid watching too much TV.

---

16    The name comes from Rudyard Kipling's 1901 novel *Kim*, in which the lead character, Kim, plays the game during his training as a spy.

# Reading and references

If I could recommend one thing to read it would be:

Deans for Impact (2015). *The Science of Learning.*

*The Science of Learning* summarises cognitive science research on how students learn, and connects it to practical implications for teaching. The report is a resource for anyone interested in how learning takes place. It presents six key questions about learning.

'To learn, students must transfer information from working memory (where it is consciously processed) to long-term memory (where it can be stored and later retrieved),' the report says. 'Students have limited working memory capacities that can be overwhelmed by tasks that are cognitively too demanding. Understanding new ideas can be impeded if students are confronted with too much information at once.'

## References

101. *Did you know?*: Miller, G. A. (1956) 'The magical number seven, plus or minus two: some limits on our capacity for processing information', *Psychological Review*, 63 (2), pp.81–97.

104. *'TV viewing may actually diminish our short-term memory capacity, damaging development'*: Canadian Paediatric Society (2017) 'Screen time and young children: promoting health and development in a digital world', *Paediatrics & Child Health*, 22 (8), pp.461–477.

## Other general references for this chapter

Gilchrist, A. L., Cowan, N. and Naveh-Benjamin, M. (2008) 'Working memory capacity for spoken sentences decreases with adult ageing: recall of fewer but not smaller chunks in older adults', *Memory*, 16 (7), pp.773–87.

New South Wales Department for Education, *Cognitive load theory in practice: examples for the classroom*, Centre for Education, Statistics and Evaluation.

Pashler, H., Bain, P., Bottge, B., Graesser, A., Koedinger, K., McDaniel, M. and Metcalfe, J. (2007) *Organizing instruction and study to improve student learning.* National Center for Education Research, Institute of Education Sciences, US Department of Education.

Van Merriënboer, J., Kirschner, P. and Kester, L. (2003) 'Taking the load off a learner's mind: instructional design for complex learning', *Educational Psychologist*, 38 (1), pp.5–13.

Sweller, J. (1998) 'Cognitive load during problem solving: effects on learning', *Cognitive Science*, 12, pp.257–285.

Sweller, J., Ayres, P. and Kalyuga, S. (2011) *Cognitive load theory*. Springer-Verlag.

# 13. Academic selection

**Key takeaways**
- Grouping children by how well they do academically is done badly in schools.
- Don't obsess too much about whether your child gets into the top set.
- But do question decisions if they're not properly justified.

## Lifetime scars

The biggest problem with academic selection is that it's done badly. Sometimes it's due to the crude tests used to assess pupils. Sometimes it's due to poor decisions made over which pupils are selected for which sets. No teacher intends it to be this way. But the results can be hugely damaging. So many of us carry scars for life because we've been judged to be not good enough at school.

The subject never fails to rise to the surface every time I catch up with one of my oldest school friends. Forty years ago, Steve didn't make it into the top stream during our first year at secondary school. Little did we know that a test we took in the first few days after arriving at our school would shape our destiny for years to come.

We attended a state comprehensive which took in pupils from all family backgrounds in the local area. For the next five years we remained in the same sets, based on the results of that one exam. No-one moved up; no-one moved down. Four decades on, after a highly successful business career, Steve still feels a deep sense of injustice about it all. He never got a second chance to show what he could do.

Our world is filled with people like Steve who missed the academic cut, but who nonetheless went on to do amazing things in their lives. Over the years I've met a long, unlikely cast of academic rejects: a headmaster who turned around several failing schools who had failed his 11-plus exam; a multi-millionaire entrepreneur who was consigned to the bottom set at his school; and a professor of medicine who has helped to save thousands of lives who was told she was no good at maths.

Decisions made at school, sometimes on the basis of one dropped mark, can cause feelings of resentment that last a lifetime. Being seen as second best before we've had time to barely know who we are can completely shape our views for evermore. It's easy to understand why so many parents feel anxious about academic sorting, despite all the stories of successful people who didn't do well at school.

## Set ways

Schools have always grouped children by how well they perform academically. In theory at least, it makes for more efficient teaching. The idea is that it enables a teacher to focus on a narrower range of pace and content in lessons.

Before they can string two sentences together, children are put into groups. Primary school pupils judged as more advanced than others are placed on separate tables for some activities. Teachers try not to make a big deal out of it. But children immediately know where they sit in the academic pecking order.

Most secondary school pupils meanwhile are organised into separate classes or sets for subjects such as maths. Around 5% of state schools – grammars – enrol pupils who get the highest marks in 11-plus exams. Sixth form colleges and universities select students on how well they have done in their exams at age 16 and 18 respectively.

## Faulty assumptions

But academic selection isn't done well. We assume that judgements made in schools are objective. But the evidence suggests otherwise. For children, a lot comes down to their mood and luck on the day of the test. Markers are also inconsistent. One study estimated that a quarter of grades awarded in official exams at age 16 are wrong. Testing is an unreliable science.

Meanwhile teachers, like all humans, suffer from unconscious bias, unwittingly stereotyping students. It's natural that some pupils don't get on with their teachers as much as others do. Despite their best efforts, teachers tend to favour those they like, or those who have neater handwriting.

You only have to look at the backgrounds of children in top academic sets to know something isn't quite right. Pupils from poorer homes are conspicuous by their absence. Is this because they are all inherently less clever, or could it be that they haven't been given extra help and tutoring support?

Why is it that so many summer-born children are found languishing in 'low-ability' sets? Do we really believe that being born in August makes you less capable than being born in September? Schools don't really test children for their ability; they assess capability at a point in time, based on how well pupils perform in a one-off (unreliable) test.

Research shows that this is a zero-sum game. The extra progress observed for higher achievers flourishing in the top sets is offset by the damage done to pupils who do worse in the bottom classes. The more extreme the selection is, the bigger the academic divide it opens up between education's haves and have-nots.

Our biggest problem is that children, teachers and parents fall into the trap of thinking that academic ability can be identified easily, and that this talent is fixed forever, immutable to any change. Ability grouping crushes the self-belief of pupils who feel that no amount of hard work will allow them to escape from the bottom of the class.

Academic selection appears to bring little benefit to classroom teaching. Teachers are tricked into thinking that pupils in the same set are at similar levels, and that large gaps in learning exist between different classes. However, research shows that there is a huge range of different needs and levels within the same sets. A teacher can underestimate these differences, failing to differentiate teaching enough for each individual pupil. The pace of lessons can be too fast for some pupils in the 'high-ability' groups, and too slow in the 'low-ability' groups.

## What you can do

There are two important messages for parents. The first is not to obsess too much about whether your son or daughter gets into the top set. It may seem like a life-and-death decision at the time. But if managed well, it needn't be a concern at all. Often it's the parents of children who get fixated on which set their children are in rather than the children themselves. The most damaging thing for children is their parents' anxieties.

At the same time, it's perfectly reasonable to question and challenge decisions if they haven't been properly justified or thought through by schools. I've observed poor practice many times. If schools do organise pupils in sets, they should have a clear and objective rationale for how they are making their academic judgements.

There should be flexible arrangements so that pupils can move up and down sets across different subjects.

## Big-fish-little-pond effect

You may think that the top set is the best place to be for your son or daughter. But that is not necessarily the case. One reason is what's called the big-fish-little-pond effect (BFLPE). Researchers have found that students ranked lowly in top academic sets suffer from lower academic confidence than similar students in lower sets.

The reason for this is that we tend to judge ourselves relative to the people around us. If you're one of the lowest achievers in a class, you have less belief in your own abilities. If you're one of the highest achievers in the class, you have more self-belief. The BFLPE punctures the assumption that all children benefit from being selected into a top set or from gaining admission into a highly selective school. The effect has been documented across all ages, from primary schools to universities. More anxious students experience larger effects.

## Focus on personal improvement

Try to get your children to think like sports professionals improving their personal bests, rather than comparing themselves with others in the class (see chapter 5). It's so easy to get hung up on whether your child is lagging behind their high-performing classmate. It's far better to focus on how they are improving over time, valuing their efforts to do better.

## Flexible approach to setting

We may think that children improve their understanding and knowledge in a steady, linear way. But in fact children develop in different ways at different times. Some are early starters; others flourish at later ages. A key question to ask teachers is how they are allowing children to move in and out of sets. The sets must be fluid.

Also, are they grouping different pupils for different subjects? Just because someone is high-achieving in maths, doesn't mean they're also high-achieving in English. Students' capabilities must be constantly reassessed. And why is the school setting in some subjects but not others?

## Teachers matter most

Debates will forever rage about whether we should have setting or mixed-ability classes in schools. But what really matters is how children are taught after they have been assigned to different classrooms. Is your child benefiting from high-quality instruction and feedback for their specific learning needs?

Often the most effective teaching – problem-solving and critical thinking – is more likely to occur in the top sets. Teachers in low sets can spend more time on managing behaviour in the classroom. Is your school assigning the most effective teachers to the bottom sets, where they are needed the most?

**Five bits of advice**

- Remember the big-fish-little-pond effect – children may gain greater confidence from being highly ranked in a lower set.
- Children should focus on personal improvement, not how they compare with peers.
- Are teachers adopting a flexible approach to setting, re-assessing students' progress?
- How are teachers catering for your children's particular learning challenges?
- Is your teacher able to spend time on problem-solving and thinking skills rather than managing behaviour?

# Reading and references

If I could recommend one thing to read it would be:

Boaler J., Wiliam, D. and Brown, M. (2000) 'Students' experiences of ability grouping – disaffection, polarisation and the construction of failure', *British Educational Research Journal*, 26 (5), pp.631–648.

This research paper is unusual in reporting what students think about setting in schools. The researchers followed 14- and 15-year-olds grouped into different maths classes in six schools. They found that students in lower sets were restricted in their learning. Many students in top sets could not keep up with the pace of learning. Almost all of the students interviewed from 'setted groups' were unhappy with their placement.

'The traditional British concern with ensuring that some of the ablest students reach the highest possible standards appears to have resulted in a situation in which the vast majority of students achieve well below their potential,' concludes the paper. 'As one student poignantly remarked: "Obviously we're not the cleverest, we're group 5, but still – it's still maths, we're still in year 9, we've still got to learn."'

## References

107.   *Did you know?*: Marsh, H. W., Seaton, M., Trautwein, U., Lüdtke, O., Hau, K. T., O'Mara, A. J. and Craven, R. G. (2008) 'The big-fish–little-pond-effect stands up to critical scrutiny: implications for theory, methodology, and future research', *Educational Psychology Review*, 20 (3), pp.319–350.

108.   *'a quarter of grades awarded in official exams at age 16 are wrong'*: Rhead, S., Black, B. and Pinot de Moira, A. (2020) *Marking consistency metrics: an update*. Ofqual.

109.   *The extra progress observed for higher achievers is offset by the damage done to pupils who do worse in the bottom classes*: Gamoran, A. (1992) 'Synthesis of research: is ability grouping equitable?', *Educational Leadership*, 50, pp.11–17.

109.   *'there is a huge range of different needs and levels within the same sets'*: Elliot Major, L. and Higgins, S. (2019) *What works? Research and evidence for successful teaching*. Bloomsbury.

110.   *'students ranked lowly in top academic sets suffer from lower academic confidence'*: Marsh, H. W., Seaton, M., Trautwein, U., Lüdtke, O., Hau, K. T., O'Mara, A. J. and Craven, R. G. (2008) 'The big-fish–little-pond-effect stands up to critical scrutiny: implications for theory, methodology, and future research', *Educational Psychology Review*, 20 (3), pp.319–350.

See also: Fang, J., Huang, X., Zhang, M., Huang, F., Li, Z. and Yuan, Q. (2018) 'The big-fish-little-pond effect on academic self-concept: a meta-analysis', *Frontiers in Psychology*, 9, 1569.

110.   *'The effect has been documented across all ages'*: Marsh, H. W., Seaton, M., Trautwein, U., Lüdtke, O., Hau, K. T., O'Mara, A. J. and Craven, R. G. (2008) 'The big-fish–little-pond-effect stands up to critical scrutiny: implications for theory, methodology, and future research', *Educational Psychology Review*, 20 (3), pp.319–350.

## Other general references for this chapter

Gutiérrez, R. and Slavin, R. E. (1992) 'Achievement effects of the nongraded elementary school: a best evidence synthesis', *Review of Educational Research*, 62 (4), pp.333–376.

Puzio, K. and Colby, G. (2010) *The effects of within class grouping on reading achievement: a meta-analytic synthesis*. Society for Research on Educational Effectiveness.

Roy, P., Styles, B., Walker, M., Morrison, J., Nelson, J. and Kettlewell, K. (2018) *Best practice in grouping students intervention A: best practice in setting*. Education Endowment Foundation.

# 14. Digital dilemmas

**Did you know?**

Between 2005 and 2015, the amount of time British children spent online more than doubled: in 2005, 8- to 15-year-olds went online 6.2 hours per week; in 2015, the average was 15 hours.

**Key takeaways**

- Try to ensure your children's screen time helps rather than hinders their learning.
- Engaging with your children about their screen use is likely to be more effective than enforcing limits on their screen time.
- There are many websites that can boost learning, but these should complement rather than replace face-to-face teaching.

## Jekyll and Hyde

One of modern-day parenting's most pressing questions is how to ensure that our children's screen time helps rather than hinders their learning.

You can understand why parents suffer from a Jekyll and Hyde attitude when it comes to the all-conquering invasion of smartphones, laptops and social media. Some days the technological age feels like our worst nightmare. On others, this brave new digital world is creating educational wonders past generations could only dream about.

So many parents I know suffer sleepless nights over their digital dilemmas. They are battered and bruised from bitter clashes trying to wrestle their zoned-out children away from game consoles. They are worn down by endless rows trying to persuade their sons and daughters to remove their headphones when doing their homework. They are sick with worry about their young children seeing explicit pornographic content.

Surveys show that two thirds of parents want to limit their children's screen time. Imposing daily allowances or restricting internet use to particular apps feel like desperate measures in a battle already lost. Half of infants between 6 and 11 months use a touchscreen daily.

Our attempts to control screen time are deploying outdated tactics for a bygone era when the world has already moved on. We are already in the digital age. Those of us who were born before the internet existed still think of computers and phones as new arrivals; for digital natives like our children they define the way we live, learn, and interact with others.

At the same time, we can barely keep up with the accelerating pace of developments in digital learning. Some predict an education future in which children's learning will be as much about online interactions as it is face-to-face classroom teaching. The best apps and websites have the potential to engage and motivate students and personalise their learning.

## Stop watching the clock

Some of the best advice to help us through our digital dilemmas comes from Sonia Livingstone and Alicia Blum-Ross, two psychologists based at the London School of Economics.

In their book *Parenting for a Digital Future*, they argue it's time for parents to adopt a different approach. Instead of policing children's screen time through rules and warnings, we would be better off engaging with our children to discuss how they can use the internet safely and effectively.

The only way to manage, according to Livingstone and Blum-Ross, is to focus on 'what is the content, who are you connecting with, what are the child's needs?' This is good advice for navigating our children's digital learning. Rather than watching the clock, we need to manage the time.

## Future skills

We must also remind ourselves that the skills our children are picking up on their consoles, computers and phones are likely preparing them for a future we can't yet imagine, for jobs that have not yet been created, and for technologies that have not yet been invented. If you are worried about their obsession with video games, then try to keep an open mind on what life-saving skills your children may be picking up.

Just one unexpected example came up when a 78-year-old relation had to undergo an operation to address his irregular heartbeat. Being on local anaesthetic, John was able to observe the modern wonders of surgery.

Doctors threaded a flexible tube into a large vein in his leg up into the heart. The tip of the catheter was then used to emit short bursts of energy to destroy tiny patches of heart tissue causing the arrhythmia. While one doctor scanned images to detect heartbeat spikes on his computer screen, another zapped the errant cells with his joystick.

Afterwards, the young doctor said how his parents had once castigated him for gaming into the early morning hours when he was younger. Now they were just proud of what he does. Modern medicine is just one example of how we are being transported into a futuristic world that none of us are able to predict.

At the same time, we also need to keep things in perspective. Concerns have been raised that surgery students are now less competent and less confident in using their hands. They have spent so much time in front of screens that they have lost the dexterity for stitching or sewing up patients.

## Education value

In education, blended learning that combines online remote lessons with face-to-face teaching is fast becoming the new normal. But my research collaborator, Steve Higgins, is always quick to remind us that the rapid advance of technology has not altered the fundamentals of learning. The hard wiring of the human brain remains unchanged.

Educationalists can get very excited by new gadgets. Modern-day classrooms are awash with iPads and interactive whiteboards. But so often these shiny new toys are not used to enhance learning. The basics of learning are still the same. Children still need time to digest new concepts, receive feedback from teachers, find out what they need to learn next, and talk with their fellow pupils.

## What you can do

### Engaging, not enforcing

Rather than trying to police screen time through rules and penalties, try engaging with your children to find the best websites or apps that will benefit their learning. With so much available, ask for tips from teachers. It may be online quizzes, video lessons or websites that use gaming to try to engage children in learning. As with everything else, this can be a matter of trying out a range of options. Websites can help to nurture literacy skills like vocabulary, research, and fluency in reading.

When children are younger, try to encourage them to play games that have some educational value. Just as Lego helps children to develop mathematical skills, spatial awareness and creativity, so Minecraft encourages programming skills, teamwork and problem-solving. Be careful about using devices simply as pacifiers for young children; you will find you can never tear them away again. (Although, reassuringly, one review of studies found no link between the use of social media and poorer school grades among adolescents.)

## Diagnostic questions

As children get older, there are education websites that can help more directly with the fundamentals of learning. Some provide lists of diagnostic questions for children. These are special questions because they give much more information than merely telling us if children have got something right or wrong. They reveal why children are getting the questions wrong at the same time.

Quick-fire quizzes of multiple choice questions can be cleverly designed in this way. One of the answers will be correct. But the three incorrect answers can be chosen to reveal the common misconceptions that pupils have when approaching these types of problems. Identifying common misconceptions is a key teaching skill, and a good way of providing feedback on where children are in their learning.

## Personalised learning and assistive technologies

Some websites aim to offer personalised lessons that respond to the specific, individual needs of your children. Children are given specific tasks and provided with individual support and feedback. This acknowledges that children learn at different paces from each other. There are now many personalised learning tools available across a range of subjects.

If your children have special learning needs, there are a host of clever websites that use assistive technologies, with tools playing to their strengths and working around their challenges. They can help children overcome difficulties with reading, writing and mathematics as well as learning and study skills.

## Teacher questions

Ask teachers how their use of technology is helping them meet their learning goals in school. So often iPads are introduced into classrooms because it's thought that they are good for children, but they aren't used for specific learning aims. What education challenges are they seeking to address? What websites and applications are used at school that are accessible for children from home? Does the school use text messages to update parents on their children's progress?

What is their policy towards mobile phones? Research has confirmed our worst fears about the distractions of this technology: schools in England that ban mobile phones see better academic results afterwards.[17]

## Get off your own screens!

Finally, are you practising what you preach? It's easy to fall into the trap of encouraging our children to manage their screen time, while at the same time spending too much time on phones ourselves. Surveys suggest that it is the overuse of phones by parents that can disrupt family life. Explore tech-free activities together. These novel experiences in the digital age can improve family relationships. They can also be good fun.

### Five bits of advice

- Rather than watching the clock, manage your child's screen time.
- Spend time with your children to explore which websites are good for their learning.
- Assistive technology tools can help children with learning needs.
- Ask teachers how their use of technology is helping them meet their learning goals.
- Explore digital detox activities together.

---

17 The ban had the most impact on students with special educational needs and those eligible for free school meals, but no discernible effect on high achievers.

# Reading and references

If I could recommend one thing to read it would be:

US Office of Educational Technology (2020) *Parent and Family Digital Learning Guide.*

This is a useful guide for parents showing how technology can help children's learning, with lots of practical advice. It aims to help all parents, from those who have limited experience with digital tools to those who know a lot, and anywhere in between. 'Technology and digital tools can help your child learn in ways that work for your child,' says the guide. 'These tools can help change the way content is presented and how learning is assessed. They can make instruction personalized based on what will help your child learn.'

## References

115.   *Did you know?/'two thirds of parents want to limit their children's screen time*': Blum-Ross, A. and Livingstone, S. (2016) *Families and screen time: current advice and emerging research.* Media Policy Brief 17. London School of Economics and Political Science.

116.   *'Half of infants between 6 and 11 months use a touchscreen daily*': Cheung, C., Bedford, R., Saez De Urabain, I., Karmiloff-Smith, A. and Smith, T. (2017) 'Daily touchscreen use in infants and toddlers is associated with reduced sleep and delayed sleep onset', *Scientific Reports,* 7 (1).

116.   *'what is the content, who are you connecting with, what are the child's needs?'*: Blum-Ross, A. and Livingstone, S. (2016) *Families and screen time: current advice and emerging research.* Media Policy Brief 17. London School of Economics and Political Science.

117.   *'surgery students are now less competent and less confident in using their hands*': Coughlan, S. (2018) 'Surgery students "losing dexterity to stitch patients"', *BBC News,* 30 October.

118.   *'no link between the use of social media and poorer school grades among adolescents*': Appel, M., Marker, C., and Gnambs, T. (2020) 'Are social media ruining our lives? A review of meta-analytic evidence', *Review of General Psychology,* 24 (1), pp.60–74.

119.   *'schools in England that ban mobile phones see better academic results*': Beland, L. and Murphy, R. (2015) *CEP discussion paper No. 1350; technology, distraction and student performance.* Centre for Economic Performance.

119.   *Overuse of phones by parents can disrupt family life*: Burns, J. (2017) 'Parents' mobile use harms family life, say secondary pupils', *BBC News,* 23 April.

## Other general references for this chapter

Cuban, L. (1993) 'Computers meet classroom: classroom wins', *Teachers College Record*, 95 (2), pp.185–210.

Higgins, S., Xiao, Z., and Katsipataki, M. (2012) *The impact of digital technology on learning*. Education Endowment Foundation.

Zosh, J. M., Hopkins, E. J., Jensen, H., Liu, C., Neale, D., Hirsh-Pasek, K., Solis, S. L. and Whitebread (2017) *Learning through play: a review of the evidence*. The Lego Foundation.

# 15. Seeking feedback

**Did you know?**

Pupils spend as much as 80% of their time pretending to listen in class.

**Key takeaways**
- It's difficult for teachers to cater for the specific learning needs of every pupil in their class.
- Effective individualised feedback is one of the best ways of improving learning.
- Excessive praise for children can do more harm than good.

## Teaching's impossible challenge

Professor Graham Nuthall exposed an uncomfortable truth at the heart of classroom teaching. He revealed something no-one wanted to hear, and paid a heavy price for doing so. Just like the neglected classroom pupils who Nuthall studied, he felt ostracised and ignored – a world apart from other education researchers at the time.[18]

But since he died in 2004, Nuthall's status as an education visionary has grown. One school branded him 'the most important education researcher we have never heard of'. Every teacher, and parent, should know about his work.

---

18    Nuthall saw himself as 'standing on an isolated hill'.

Over 40 years, Nuthall and his team of researchers in New Zealand undertook one of the most detailed investigations into the minute-by-minute interactions between pupils and teachers. Using microphones, video cameras, and observations, they compiled a picture of what actually happens in the classroom. Nuthall's quest was to find the most successful teaching methods that all teachers could adopt. This is like seeking educational nirvana: it would mean that all pupils would do well at school, whatever school they happened to be attending.

But after years of painstaking investigations, Nuthall abandoned his work. He was so fed up that he took up painting instead. What seemed to work for one teacher in one classroom didn't work for another teacher in another classroom. Findings from other researchers were found to be contradictory and inconsistent. His own work came under fierce attack.[19] A crestfallen Nuthall came to the reluctant conclusion that research on teaching could never produce reliable and replicable results that would be helpful for teachers.

But then came Nuthall's aha moment. He realised that learning is unique to each individual pupil. Students live in a personal world of their own in the classroom, and each one takes away something different from a lesson. 'They whisper to each other and pass notes,' explained Nuthall in a lecture he gave in 2001. 'They spread rumours about girlfriends and boyfriends, they organise their after-school social life, continue arguments that started in the playground. They care more about how their peers evaluate their behaviour than they care about the teacher's judgement.'

Nuthall had unearthed teaching's impossible challenge: in a classroom of 25 to 30 pupils, teachers are simply unable to cater for the specific learning needs of every pupil. Each learner has different histories, interests and motivations. Personal conversations with each pupil would be needed to find out exactly what steps they need to move their learning on. Instead, teachers resort to the same rituals to manage the class as a whole. Nuthall found that teachers are largely unaware of what their students are learning. They are fooled into thinking that a busy classroom equates to lots of learning taking place.

## Individualised feedback

I love revealing Nuthall's nuggets of research, whether lecturing to trainee teachers or giving public talks to groups of experienced headteachers. They always

---

19    To this day, battles between researchers continue as to how to best investigate evidence in the classroom, with extreme views on both sides. Some argue that what goes on in the classroom can be identified and generalised in a scientific way, while others argue that it's impossible to generalise as each and every classroom is a unique interaction between a teacher and their pupils.

cause a stir. Nuthall found that pupils in the class already know 40–50% of what teachers teach: that's a huge waste of effort during lessons. Meanwhile, 80% of the feedback pupils receive is from fellow pupils; and 80% of this is wrong! Nuthall also discovered the 'rule of three': students need to be taught a concept three times before it embeds in their long-term memory.

One last finding always generates a gasp among educators: what do pupils spend 80% of their time doing in class? I'm sure you can guess. It's pretending to listen. Children are brilliant pretenders. In his 2007 book *The Hidden Lives of Learners*, Nuthall recounts the tactics played out in classrooms across the world. Pupils will act as if they are trying to read a book as a teacher approaches, only to idly look out the window as soon as the teacher moves on.[20] Even the best teachers don't have eyes in the back of their heads. They just aren't able to see what the children are doing most of the time.

Nuthall's insights, alongside hundreds of other studies, have shown that providing individualised feedback is one of the best ways of improving children's progress. Feedback is information given to the learner and/or the teacher about the learner's performance relative to their learning goals, which can then redirect actions to achieve the goal. It's the second step in the teaching process after new material has been introduced. Effective feedback makes learning more efficient by changing what teachers and learners do next.

There is so much room for improving this aspect of teaching. Well delivered, it can lead to an extra three to four months extra learning gain in just one academic year. Too many children suffer from being hidden learners. And there are some simple things that parents can do to help.

# What you can do

## Three feedback questions

'How did you get on at school today?' is the standard question we tend to ask our children following our own long day at work. If we are trying to engage with teenagers in particular, we'll be lucky to get more than a grunt in response.

If you want to get a better sense of your child's progress, you should ask instead three simple questions.

- What are you doing well in your subject/at school?
- What do you need to do to improve your work in the subject/at school?
- Has your teacher given you feedback that has helped you to progress?

---

20   *The Hidden Lives of Learners* was compiled by Graham Nuthall's wife Jill after his death.

It's important to find out whether your son or daughter is getting any feedback at all. I think of two types of pupils. Some are riding on the crest of a learning wave, adept at navigating the classroom, with all the momentum behind them. Teachers often look to these prominent learners to affirm that learning has taken place for the whole class. Anyone who has stood up and taught will understand that it's completely natural to do this. But there are other pupils who are lost at sea, sinking, increasingly detached from the learning that is meant to be going on.

You need to be careful here. Effective feedback is about getting things just right – not too much, not too little. Learning is as much to do with the heart as it is to do with the head. Students face several threats to their wellbeing when considering leaps in learning, such as the fear of losing face in front of their peers or getting a question wrong. When it comes to leaps in learning, we need to adhere to the Goldilocks principle.

The teacher has to set (or agree with the learner) the right level of challenge. Too easy and the pupil may not need to try hard (or will not value positive feedback if they succeed); too difficult and no amount of effort will let them succeed (and may damage their confidence if the task ends in failure). Knowing how your child feels about their feedback (if they are getting any), and engaging with their teacher about this process will be invaluable.

The key is to focus on self-improvement rather than comparisons with classmates. Children need clear next steps. They need to know how they have improved. Remember, this should be a two-way process involving both learner and teacher. It should be a conversation, always ongoing, between teacher and pupil, about how the pupil is making progress. The ultimate aim of feedback is to create independent learners (see chapter 11).

## Marking – quality not quantity matters

You might think that marking your children's work is one of the most important things that teachers can do to help them with their learning. But once again, the research challenges this common assumption among parents. The problem is that most marking doesn't include information that enables children to do something different as a result.

Marking only helps when it contains feedback. Children just see marks as judgements on their ability. And when teachers provide comments, it's only when children act on them that they become useful. You should not worry about the quantity of marking that your son and daughter receives, but the quality of feedback that genuinely moves their learning on. They may be receiving verbal feedback in the classroom not seen in their books.

## Selective praise

One of the hardest lessons for parents who want the best for their children is to cut down on excessive praise. It's so tempting to think that showering children with positive words will help them.

The evidence, however, suggests the opposite. Praise is valued more when it is meaningful and less frequent. Children value being praised if they think they deserve it. Too much praise can backfire, suggesting that you have low expectations. It also creates unrealistic expectations of life in the workplace.

Those well-worn phrases – 'you're such a clever girl', 'you're brilliant' – should be reserved for special occasions. It's better to praise a child's effort than make generalised judgements about them as a person. The problem is that these comments provide no information for moving them on in their learning. Be specific.

### Five bits of advice

- Remember the 'rule of three': children need to be taught something three times before it embeds in their long-term memory.
- Ask your child what they think they are doing well at school, and how they might improve.
- Focus on self-improvement rather than comparison with classmates.
- It's not the quantity of marking that matters, but the quality of feedback that moves children's learning on.
- Praise your children sparingly, and tell them why they have done well.

# Reading and references

If I could recommend one thing to read it would be:

Nuthall, G. (2007) *The Hidden Lives of Learners*. NZCER Press.

This book lays bare the truth of what really happens in classrooms. Hundreds of hours of videotape evidence exposed the crude inefficiencies of everyday teaching: 50% of what teachers teach, children already know; 80% of pupils' time is spent pretending to listen; teachers talk 75% of the time.

This book shows why effective feedback is so key to learning. Nuthall also explains the 'rule of three': 'We discovered that a student needed to encounter, on at least three different occasions, the complete set of the information she or he needed to understand a concept. If the information was incomplete, or not experienced on three different occasions, the student did not learn the concept.'

## References

123. *Did you know?*: Nuthall, G. (2007) *The hidden lives of learners*. NZCER Press.

123. *'the most important education researcher we have never heard of'*: Sudbury Beach School (2016) *Graham Nuthall, the most important education researcher we never heard of.*

124. *'They whisper to each other and pass notes'*: Nuthall, G. (2001) 'The cultural myths and the realities of teaching and learning', The Jean Herbison Lecture, University of Canterbury.

125. *Feedback can lead to an extra three to four months extra learning gain*: Elliot Major, L. and Higgins, S. (2019) *What works? Research and evidence for successful teaching*. Bloomsbury.

126. *'the research challenges this common assumption'*: Elliott, V., Baird, J., Hopfenbeck, T. N., Ingram, J., Thompson, I., Usher, N., Zantout, M., Richardson, J. and Coleman, R. (2016) *A marked improvement? A review of the evidence on written marking.* Education Endowment Foundation.

127. *'Praise is valued more when it is meaningful and less frequent'*: Dweck, C. (1999) 'Caution – praise can be dangerous', *American Educator.*

## Other general references for this chapter

Australian Institute for Teaching and School Leadership, *Spotlight: reframing feedback to improve teaching and learning.*

Black, P. and Wiliam, D. (1998) 'Assessment and classroom learning', *Assessment in Education: Principles, Policy and Practice*, 5 (1), pp.7–74.

Black, P. and Wiliam, D. (2010) 'Inside the black box: raising standards through classroom assessment', *Phi Delta Kappan*, 92 (1), pp.81–90.

Hargreaves, E. (2011) 'Teachers' feedback to pupils: "Like so many bottles thrown out to sea?"', in Berry, R. and Adamson, B. (eds.) *Assessment reform in education*, pp.121–133. Springer.

Hattie, J. and Clarke, S. (2018) *Visible learning: feedback*. Routledge.

Hattie, J. and Timperley, H. (2007) 'The power of feedback', *Review of Educational Research*, 77 (1), pp.81–112.

Higgins, S. (2014) 'Formative assessment and feedback to learners', in Slavin, R. (ed.) *Classroom management & assessment*. Corwin Press.

# 16. Mind matters: learning styles and other myths

---

**Did you know?**

Over nine in ten teachers believe that people learn better when they receive information in their preferred learning style.

---

**Key takeaway**
- Your children may think they have learning preferences, but there is no evidence they help learning.

## Learning styles

You need to be on your guard for the many unfounded claims that lurk in the world of learning. Some are due to innocent misreadings of research. But education is also prey to modern-day snake oil salesmen exploiting our yearning to improve learning. They offer easy answers and quick wins, sprinkling scientific terms across their marketing materials. Most have no scientific basis whatsoever. And many can harm, not help, our children's learning.

One of the most contentious concepts is learning styles. This is the idea that we can all be classified as visual, auditory or kinaesthetic learners. A visual learner understands things better if they are presented as pictures, charts or moving images. An auditory learner responds more to spoken words and storytelling than written exercises. A kinaesthetic learner finds it hard to sit still, needing to move about during a lesson. Knowing your preference, we are told, helps you to learn better.

What would say your child's preferred learning style is?

A. Visual

B. Auditory

C. Kinaesthetic

D. All of the above

E. None of the above

As you may have found in answering this question, learning styles make a lot of intuitive sense. But this is a topic on which studies are in complete agreement: teaching children in their preferred learning styles doesn't improve their exam results. Children who say they prefer learning visually – 'visualisers' – are no more likely to remember pictures than other children. Children who say they prefer learning verbally – 'verbalisers' – are no better at remembering spoken words. This probably means the safest answer to the question of whether your child has a particular learning style is E: they have none.

But the idea of learning styles persists, among teachers as well as others. For example, one survey found that nine in ten teachers (93%) believe that people learn better when they receive information in their preferred learning style. Perhaps this assumption is so persistent because, like many education myths, there is a grain of truth to it.

It's true that children learn differently. They are good at different things. Some are naturally creative; some are born with a good ear for music; others are gifted with strong spatial awareness. But it's a big leap to define children by an overall preferred style of learning, and then claim that this will help improve their academic grades.

This alluring idea has had catastrophic effects on children's lives. The most notorious example of recent times was the rebuilding of schools in the borough of Knowsley in 2009, following a local council audit that concluded that most local children were kinaesthetic learners. Despite protests from teachers, classrooms and corridors were replaced by vast open spaces designed for children to move around in rather than sitting down behind desks.

Pupils dubbed the buildings 'wacky warehouses'. Exam results were the only things that remained unchanged, stuck at the foot of the national league tables. Thousands of children left school with few or no qualifications.

Daniel Willingham, a cognitive psychologist at the University of Virginia, has reluctantly become the world's leading debunker of learning styles. He's been trying to puncture the myth for so many years he's become sick of writing about it. 'Students may have preferences about how to learn,' he concludes. 'But no evidence suggests that catering to those preferences will lead to better learning.'

A key point here is that any labelling is dangerous. The danger is that children are stereotyped and restricted in their learning. This is a particular concern for younger children. They may come to believe that any lack of progress is due to their learning style, which can't be changed.

Presenting ideas in different ways can also be helpful for learners. Combining pictures and sounds can enhance learning, increasing the capacity of our working memory. And different tasks require different types of learning. Being able to visualise is useful for studying maths as well as art, for example.

For parents, the advice is clear. Challenge your children to think of the best way to tackle a task. Plan different ways to explain complex ideas. But do not limit them by what you or they think is their style.

The idea of learning styles is not the only education myth to watch out for. There are many 'brain training' outfits now on the block aiming to exploit the burgeoning interest in findings from cognitive science. Scientific terms are sprinkled across their marketing materials. Unsubstantiated claims are made about improving working memory capacity.

For example, 'learning pyramids' apparently show how much people remember of what they hear, read and see. These percentages are pure fiction. 'Brain Gym' is the name of a programme based on the idea that moving leads to optimal learning for children – termed 'educational kinesiology'. The founders claim the programme can help improve memory, concentration and intelligence. But this is backed by zero evidence.

## Five bits of advice

- Learning styles is an enticing idea but with zero evidence that it helps learning.
- Labelling children is dangerous as it can limit them.
- Combining pictures and sounds can enhance learning.
- Be sceptical of brain-training programmes (particularly those asking for money).
- Be on your guard for education myths!

# Reading and references

If I could recommend one thing to read it would be:

Willingham, D. (2018) 'Ask the cognitive scientist: does tailoring instruction to "learning styles" help students learn?', *American Educator,* 42 (2), pp.28–32.

This is an interview with the psychologist Daniel Willingham on the insights but also limitations of cognitive science in improving how children learn. He discusses the myth that school is designed for left-brained students, and the myth that young children's brains must have lots of sensory stimulation – and that classical music is especially important.

'A deep understanding of the brain will come, hand-in-hand, with a deep understanding of the mind, and that is bound to help education,' argues Willingham. 'There is not, however, any prospect of a brain-based learning program of any substance in the near future.'

## References

131.  *Did you know?*: Howard-Jones, P. A. (2014) 'Neuroscience and education: myths and messages', *Nature Reviews Neuroscience,* 15, pp.817–824.

132.  *'teaching children in their preferred learning styles doesn't improve their exam results'*: Riener, C. R. and Willingham, D. T. (2010) 'The myth of learning styles', *Change: the magazine of higher learning,* 42 (5), pp.32–35.

132.  *Rebuilding of schools in* Knowsley: Cobain, I. (2017) 'The making of an education catastrophe', *The Guardian,* 29 January.

133.  *'Students may have preferences about how to learn'*: Riener, C. R. and Willingham, D. T. (2010) 'The myth of learning styles', *Change: the magazine of higher learning,* 42 (5), pp.32–35.

## Other general references for this chapter

Geake, J. (2008) 'Neuromythologies in education', *Educational Research,* 50 (2), pp.123–133.

Goswami, U. (2006) 'Neuroscience and education: from research to practice?', *Nature Reviews Neuroscience,* 7, pp.406–413.

Pashler, H., McDaniel, M., Rohrer, D. and Bjork, R. (2008) 'Learning styles: concepts and evidence', *Psychological Science in the Public Interest,* 9 (3), pp.105–119.

Waterhouse, L. (2006) 'Multiple intelligences, the Mozart effect, and emotional intelligence: a critical review', *Educational Psychologist,* 41 (4), pp.207–225.

Watson, A. and Kelso, G. L. (2014) 'The effect of Brain Gym on academic engagement for children with developmental disabilities', *International Journal of Special Education*, 29 (2).

# 17. Exploring apprenticeships

**Did you know?**

Taking an apprenticeship can lead to a much higher salary than many graduates will earn, with the added benefit of no student debts.

**Key takeaways**

- Despite their many benefits, vocational routes suffer from uninformed snobbery.
- We are witnessing a renaissance in apprenticeships with many high-quality opportunities now available.
- Finding a good apprenticeship takes a lot of work and research.

## The dinner table test

It is a brave parent who tells their friends over dinner that their daughter or son has chosen to do an apprenticeship instead of a degree. Up until recently, this news would be greeted with awkward pauses and polite smiles. The 'dinner table test' sums it up well: middle-class Brits have for too long looked down their noses at the earn-while-you-learn route. There's just something grubby about non-academic options. Technical qualifications are deemed as second class. The half of young people who don't go to university are seen as low-status also-rans.

Elsewhere around the globe it couldn't be more different. In Germany, company executives are lauded for rising up from the factory floor. In Australia, teachers rejoice when their pupils leave school to begin apprenticeships. In Britain meanwhile, the term for a work-related qualification, BTEC, is used by teenagers as slang for something that is decidedly ropey. This tells you everything you need to know.

The economist Alison Wolf summed it up when she wrote that vocational qualifications are 'a great idea for other people's children'. According to England's former Education Secretary Kenneth Baker, it is pure academic snobbery — a misguided belief that technical education is about 'shabby premises and dirty jobs down in the town'.

## Benefits

But those who mock vocational training are misinformed and misguided. The stereotyped image of apprentices as males in dirty overalls doing manual trades could not be more outdated. From finance to fashion, from technology to beauty therapy, from policing to engineering, to electricians, sheet-metal workers, caterers, barbers and solicitors, apprenticeships span most walks of working life.

Taking a paid job that includes training, moreover, can lead to much higher salaries than other school leavers, with the added benefit of no student debts. Many degree-level apprentices earn more over their lifetimes than some graduates. One study found that 91% of apprentices go on to further study or jobs – slightly higher than the 89% of university graduates who did so.

Many parents may not even know that there are such things as Higher National Certificates and Higher National Diplomas. These sub-degree qualifications are another vocational option. They take one to two years in college and focus on 'learning by doing'. They provide skills that you can use in a particular job. Taken in subjects such as science, technology, engineering and mathematics, they too can lead to higher earnings than many graduates are earning several years after leaving university.

## A renaissance in apprenticeships

You can now reel off these impressive statistics next time you're at the dinner table. They are certainly turning heads in high places. Many private schools now list apprenticeships alongside the academic destinations of their pupils. Several prestigious universities enrol thousands of students on degree apprenticeships enabling them to train with employers. Blue-chip companies are diverting resources into apprenticeship programmes rather than graduate schemes. We are witnessing a renaissance in apprenticeships.[21]

---

21    Apprenticeships were first regulated in 1562 in an Act of Parliament of England called The Statute of Artificers, under Queen Elizabeth I.

Rising tuition fees are prompting second thoughts about whether all university degrees are worth the money, particularly when compared with the growing possibilities to 'earn while you learn'. I've known so many young people who ended up deeply unhappy doing a degree because they felt it was something that they were expected to do. More school leavers are now looking to alternative paths. And apprenticeships have the added advantage that you don't have to pay anything towards your qualification.

Dare I say it, many apprenticeships have developed a certain cache. One study found that American parents now value a Google internship over a Harvard degree. Degree study is all well and good, but at the end of the day we parents want jobs and careers for our children.[22]

# What you can do

Here is what I would advise young people considering an apprenticeship, with help from their parents. Work alongside them to ensure they do their research and make informed choices.

## Do your homework

Let's be clear: opting out of academic study means more work. You will have to take the lead to do the research and assess the many choices available. There is a huge variety of apprenticeships and vocational courses – that's both an advantage and disadvantage.

Apprenticeships come in four types: intermediate (level 2, equivalent to 5 GCSEs); advanced (level 3, equivalent to 2 A-levels); higher (levels 4–7, equivalent to a certificate of higher education or foundation degree all the way up to a master's degree); and degree (levels 6–7, equivalent to a bachelor's or master's degree).

Pursuing the vocational pathway instead of the well-trodden and signposted 'royal route' of university education is a bit like going off-road into an uncertain but exciting terrain. Many schools are still failing to tell their students about apprenticeships.

There is no central applications system as there is for university degrees. You and your child will need to search jobs websites and information provided by employers. It will feel more like applying for a job than a university degree. It's down to parents to help navigate a path forward in an ever expanding space. There are new apprenticeships in more specialist fields coming up all the time, from cyber security to space engineering to nuclear science.

---

22   In a 2020 survey, 57% of parents thought that apprenticeships offered a better chance of getting a good job than university. The survey was undertaken by the Chartered Management Institute (CMI).

## Explore degree apprenticeships

I strongly recommend exploring the option of degree apprenticeships. Several prestigious universities have teamed up with national employers from the BBC to Jaguar Land Rover to BT, to develop courses where your time is split between university and work.

For some school leavers they are the best of both worlds. They'll be paid a wage by their employer throughout the course. They'll graduate with a bachelor's degree or a master's degree. They'll develop expertise in fascinating subjects, from psychological wellbeing to diagnostic radiography to data science. At the same time, they will develop transferable skills and gain work experience that will distinguish them from graduates.

Even if they choose to leave the employer they completed their apprenticeship with, they'll be highly employable. The snag is that with relatively small numbers of courses still available, some degree apprenticeships are now as hard to get into as the most popular degree courses.

## Subject is key

Remember that what we study can be more important than the level of study in both vocational and academic education.

Apprenticeships in engineering, mostly taken up by boys, are associated with high salaries. Girls can do well in engineering too. They are often put off by the stereotypical view that these fields are male-only, and don't explore the breadth of jobs available. We need to do better in challenging these stereotypes: talk with your daughters about them. There are emerging organisations and resources who can provide some help.

Salaries also vary enormously for Higher National Certificates (HNCs) and Higher National Diplomas (HNDs) across different fields of study. Currently these sub-degree qualifications fit gender stereotypes. More than three quarters of those studying HNCs in engineering and technology, architecture, building and construction and computing are male. Meanwhile, around 70% of those studying HNDs in subjects allied to medicine (mostly nursing) are female.

## Ask about progression

If your children are enrolling on level 2 or level 3 apprenticeships, equivalent to GCSEs and A-levels, make sure there is clear progression to further training or jobs afterwards. This should be automatic. Ask employers what previous apprentices went on to do. There's no point in investing your time in training if it doesn't lead you on to anywhere.

## Equip them with life skills

Employers say that what they need from future employees are key life skills: the ability to communicate, character, grit and conscientiousness, determination and ambition. Many of these characteristics come from the home, not the school. Parents should think proactively about how they can ensure children use all of their experiences to learn these skills (see chapter 20).

It may seem like a cliché, but it is also true: the nature of work and jobs is changing rapidly. Parents and young people shouldn't expect a single apprenticeship, or a three-year degree for that matter, to see them through a career lasting several decades. Jobs at a single company for life are a thing of the past. Most people will need those transferable life skills to prosper in many roles.

## Consider T Levels

A brand new offering for sixth formers from 2021 onwards are T Levels, or Technical Level Qualifications. These two-year courses have been designed jointly with companies. They aim to prepare students for working life. They will be equivalent to 3 A-levels.

T Levels will offer a mixture of classroom learning and on-the-job training. Students will be able to then go on to further study at university or pursue a higher apprenticeship. As for any new qualification, the litmus test for T Levels will be how quickly they command respect among employers. These are demanding courses, designed for high-achieving school pupils.

### Five bits of advice

- Get your children to think carefully about whether the easy option of applying to university is actually the best option for them.
- Help them to do the research: selecting a good apprenticeship takes time.
- The field of study or job sector is critical in determining salary prospects afterwards.
- Look to the future: ensure there is genuine progression as part of the apprenticeship.
- Encourage them to explore degree apprenticeships, which combine the benefits of learning at university and in the workplace.

# Reading and references

If I could recommend one thing to read it would be:

Success at School, *A parent's guide to apprenticeships*.

This is a helpful guide that defines apprenticeships, goes through the different types, compares them to university routes, explores some of the programmes available, looks at how much children can expect to earn, and explains how to help find an apprenticeship.

'If you think they're second best to a university degree, you've been misinformed,' the guide says. 'Apprenticeships can be a pathway to a degree – paid for in full by the employer while your child earns a wage.'

## References

137.  *Did you know?*: Boston Consulting Group (2013) *Real apprenticeships: creating a revolution in English skills*. The Sutton Trust.

138.  *'a great idea for other people's children'*: Wolf, A. (2002) *Does education matter? Myths about education and economic growth*. Penguin.

138.  *'91% of apprentices go on to further study or jobs'*: Department for Education (2019) *Further education: outcome-based success measures, academic years 2013/14 to 2016/17*.

138.  *HNCs and HNDs can lead to higher earnings*: Cavaglia, C., McNally, S. and Ventura, G. (2020) 'Do apprenticeships pay? Evidence for England', *Oxford Bulletin of Economics and Statistics*, 82, pp.1094–1134.

139.  *'American parents now value a Google internship over a Harvard degree'*: Busteed, B. (2020) 'Americans rank a Google internship over a Harvard degree', *Forbes*, 6 January.

## Other general references for this chapter

Amazing Apprenticeships (2019), *Parents' pack: apprenticeship information*.

Chartered Management Institute (2020) *The age of apprenticeships*.

Elliot Major, L. and S. Machin (2018) *Social mobility and its enemies*. Penguin.

Espinoza Bustos, H., Speckesser, S., McNally, S., Britton, J., Tahir, I. and Vignoles, A. (2020) *Post-18 education – who is taking the different routes and how much do they earn?* London School of Economics.

Kirby, P. (2015) *Levels of success: the potential of UK apprenticeships*. The Sutton Trust.

# 18. Choosing a university degree

**Did you know?**
One in three students would choose another degree course in hindsight.

**Key takeaways**
- Students have to navigate a bafflingly complex university admissions system with 50,000 plus degree courses.
- Not all degrees lead to better job prospects and earnings.
- Choosing the right degree is one of the most important investment decisions your child and you will make.

## Wrong choices

How do your children choose the university course best suited for them? It seems like such a simple question. But it's not straightforward at all. When faced with one of the biggest decisions of their lives, so many young people make the wrong choice.

We know this from surveys of university students. Many regret their choice of degree. In 2017, one study asked university students 'if you knew what you know now, would you have chosen another course?' Over a third (34%) replied 'definitely' or 'maybe'. That's a lot of higher-education discontents. There are millions of graduates who in hindsight would have studied a different degree.

It's heartbreaking when I meet current students and recent graduates who regret their choices. For all their hard work, many feel miserable about it. Some are even embarrassed about their degrees. Looking back even a few years later, most think they were far too young and naive when they opted for their A-level subjects and made their choices.

Hundreds of thousands of students meanwhile – a fifth of university intakes – fail to finish their degrees.

These figures aren't surprising when you think of the university admissions system we have created for our 18-year-olds (as well as our mature students). At such a young age, it's hard to know exactly what you want to do with your life. It comes at the worst possible time: when you're busy trying to secure the best grades in your school exams. To make matters worse, your hormones are still going haywire.

If you ever wanted to create a system that acts to confuse, baffle and alienate, then this surely is it. Quite apart from the dizzying array of bursaries, scholarships and fee remissions on offer for 50,000 plus degree courses, and information on the likely employment prospects they may lead to, are a battery of admissions criteria deployed by universities as they try to distinguish between thousands of equally well-qualified candidates. These include personal statements, teacher recommendations, school exam grades (predicted and actual), university admissions tests, interviews, 'contextual offers' and much more.

Good-quality information, advice and guidance for school pupils are essential in such a complex world of admissions. Yet the research suggests at least half of the advice currently given in schools is inadequate, and can be poorly timed and partial.

Teachers will try to help. But their main job is to teach. Their well-meaning advice can sometimes backfire. One study found that teacher feedback on students' personal statements made them worse, not better, in the eyes of university tutors. The single most important element for admissions tutors was a paragraph of in-depth research produced by applicants on their chosen subject. This was the part teachers were most likely to suggest leaving out.

University league tables meanwhile only tell a partial story. Numbers in official print assume an authority that is not always backed up when you dig beneath the surface. All league tables are filled with questionable approximations, suspect data and arbitrary decisions.

For all these reasons and more besides, my one piece of advice to all university applicants is simple: do your own research. Dedicate time to looking over the details of different degree courses. Contact admissions tutors and academics. Attend open days. Check out virtual events and social media. Ask lots of questions. What are the normal contact hours for students? What do graduates go on to do after the degree course? What does this degree offer that's different to others in the same discipline? Encourage your children to ask themselves whether they are choosing a degree just to get into university, or is it a course they are genuinely interested in?

Choosing the right degree is one of the most important investment decisions your children will ever make. They (and you) will be paying off debts for tuition fees for years to come. Their degree stays with them for life.

Year in, year out I've observed some common mistakes made by applicants. There are major pitfalls to avoid in university admissions. And there are easy steps to improve a student's chances of getting a course that's right for them.

# What to do

The decision of which course to choose should be led by your children, with you acting more as a helpful adviser and mentor. Adopt an authoritative parent approach, encouraging them to think for themselves, rather than telling them what to do. Here is what I would advise university applicants.

### Personal statements: a memorable love letter

Students should treat their personal statement as an audition with a world-leading academic expert who loves the subject even more than they do. School teachers often miss this key point as they are not admission experts.

Schools put a lot of emphasis on what extracurricular accomplishments students have achieved. But most admissions tutors are not interested in whether they've volunteered for the local Cats Protection charity, or traipsed over the countryside to earn a Duke of Edinburgh Bronze award.[23] They want to hear about the influential books or articles they've read about in their chosen subject, and the exhibitions or lectures they've been inspired by. Encourage them to mention anything that will demonstrate their passion for the discipline they want to study.

They also need to try to make it personal. Can they say something about themselves that will make them stand out from all the other candidates the admissions tutors will read about? Good writers open with an eye-catching opening sentence and end with compelling last words. Make sure they don't leave any grammatical errors. Whatever they claim, tell them to back it up with tangible examples.

---

23   This contrasts with leading US Ivy League colleges, which put a lot of emphasis on what you have achieved outside your school study.

A teacher can also make a big difference with their own reference. The best ones are original and well written. They feel authentic. Teachers can explain why students achieved any lower than expected grades so admissions tutors can put their results into context.

## Not all degrees lead to good job prospects

Higher education is much more than just about money. But students should always consider what the likely job prospects are from their degree. They're paying significant tuition fees and will one day be trying to get a job in an increasingly competitive world.

A good degree remains a smart investment. The wage returns for degrees have held up remarkably well despite bulging numbers of graduates. But remember, these average figures mask wide variation in the wages different graduates command. For some degrees, students earn less after university than non-graduates. Should your child consider an apprenticeship option instead?

Subjects such as medicine, economics, law, maths and business deliver substantial wage premiums compared with typical graduates. Be careful not to make sweeping judgements about more unusual courses: golf management, horse management and surf science degrees can have strong links with their respective industries and proven track records of placing graduates. We have more data than ever before on graduate outcomes. If you can't find the information, ask the university directly.

## Use university league tables with care

University league tables can be useful guides, but should be used with care. The problem is that data is often old and approximate. You should only use them to make broad judgements. You might conclude that universities ranked among the top 10 or 20 institutions for a subject are among the best, but I would advise against any finer judgements.

Help your child consider what's the best fit for them. University X may be ranked in the top 10. But if university Y is in the top 20, and offers that year in the United States they've always dreamed of and which will fuel their passion for literature or politics or sociology, isn't that the better choice?

Use the background data as ammunition to help your child pose good questions when they speak with admissions tutors. Why are student satisfaction scores not as good as elsewhere? Why are employment prospects worse than last year? Does the university help to gain work experience? Remember that sometimes employers will look at the reputation of the university as a whole more than the subject your child chose to study.

## Choose school subjects with care

Students need to choose their school subjects carefully. They should aim to keep their options as wide as possible. Highly selective universities tend to prefer traditional A-level subjects including biology, chemistry, physics, English, geography, history and maths. They are less keen on more vocational A-level subjects such as law, accounting and business. Do the research.

Understand, for example, that you don't have to study law to be a lawyer. Two in five university students said they would have made better choices if they'd had better information and advice at school. Remember too that subject choice at GCSE level can impact on A-level and university choices later down the line. Encourage your children to think ahead.

Jon Beard, who spent over a decade overseeing admissions at Cambridge and knows a lot about the topic, advises university applicants to think about what they want to do after university when choosing a degree subject. If, like many 18-year-olds, they don't know what they want to do yet, they should choose a subject that they love because they will be better at it.

'Find out which universities offer those courses, and start whittling the list down based on things which are important to you, like size, location, reputation, and how the grades they want match the sort of grades you hope to get,' Jon told me. 'A good strategy is to spread your bets: think about what your grades might reasonably look like if your exams go well, but also if they don't go so well. That will create a target range: within that aim for one university to reach for, another to act as a safety net, and the others somewhere in the middle.' Applicants should be careful not to choose something so niche that it narrows their options on graduation.

One common mistake I've seen is to take too many A-levels. Remember that universities make their choices based on three A-levels only. It's better to focus on securing good grades in three subjects rather than average grades in four.

## Aim high

Finally, encourage your children to aim high. Nearly half of young people were given a place at university in 2020 with A-level grades lower than the advertised entry requirements. Students should ring the university up when they get grades below the original university offer. They may still be offered a place.

**Five bits of advice**

- Get your children to do their own research: they should dedicate lots of time to looking over the details of different degree courses.

- Encourage them to use league table data as ammunition to pose questions directly to admissions tutors.

- They should treat their personal statement as an audition with a world-leading academic.

- Think ahead with your children about which school subjects universities prefer.

- Be prepared to negotiate for a degree place when A-level grades are below the university's original offer.

# Reading and references

If I could recommend one thing to read it would be:

UCAS (2021) *Where next? What influences the choices school leavers make?*

This report shares insights into what drives student university choices, from a survey of 27,000 students. For example, one in three university applicants report first thinking about university at primary school. Students choose their degree subject before they think about the university or college they want to attend. One in five students report they could not study a university subject that interested them because they did not study the relevant subjects at school.

The report argues for earlier, broader, and personalised careers information, advice and guidance for school students.

## References

143.   *Did you know?/'Many regret their choice of degree'*: Neves, J. and Hewit, R. (2020) *Student academic experience survey*. Higher Education Policy Institute.

144.   *Hundreds of thousands of students fail to finish their degrees*: Hillman, H. (2021) *A short guide to non-continuation in UK universities*. Higher Education Policy Institute.

144.   *'at least half of the advice currently given in schools is inadequate'*: The Sutton Trust (2008) *Increasing higher education participation amongst disadvantaged young people and schools in poor communities*.

144.   *'teacher feedback on students' personal statements made them worse'*: Jones, S. (2012) *The personal statement: a fair way to assess university applicants?* The Sutton Trust.

       See also: Jones, S. (2013) 'Ensure that you stand out from the crowd: a corpus-based analysis of personal statements according to applicants' school type', *Comparative Education Review*, 57 (3), pp.397–423.

146    *'The wage returns for degrees have held up remarkably well'*: Elliot Major, L. and Machin, S. (2018) *Social mobility and its enemies*. Penguin.

146.   *'students earn less after university than non-graduates'*: Britton, J., Dearden, L., Shephard, N. and Vignoles, A. (2016) *How English domiciled graduate earnings vary with gender, institution attended, subject and socio-economic background*. Working Paper W16/06. Institute for Fiscal Studies.

       See also: Britton, J., Dearden, L., van der Erve, L. and Waltmann, B. (2020) *The impact of undergraduate degrees on lifetime earnings*. Institute for Fiscal Studies.

147.  'Students need to choose their school subjects carefully': Dilnot, C. (2018) 'The relationship between A-level subject choice and league table score of university attended: the "facilitating", the "less suitable", and the "counter-intuitive"', *Oxford Review of Education*, 44 (1), pp.118–137.

147.  'Two in five university students said they would have made better choices': UCAS (2021) *Where next? What influences the choices school leavers make?*

147.  'Nearly half of young people were given a place at university in 2020 with A-level grades lower than the advertised entry requirements': Sellgren, K. (2019) 'Half of students get degree place with lower grades', *BBC News*, 28 November.

# 19. Debunking Oxbridge myths

**Did you know?**
Less than half of secondary state school teachers would routinely advise their highest-achieving pupils to apply to Oxbridge.

**Key takeaways**
- Beware Oxbridge myths and misconceptions.
- More than anything else, Oxbridge applicants need to demonstrate their passion for their subject.
- Oxford and Cambridge are similar but not the same.

## A Cambridge education

I wish I could conjure up a real picture of my interview, somewhere in the depths of Selwyn College, Cambridge in the winter of 1985. My mind has been corrupted by too many clichéd images of Oxbridge in the 35 years since. I can only imagine a laughably stereotyped scene: two bespectacled dons in gowns, comfy chairs, lined walls of bookshelves, oak wood panels, small windows overlooking a green quad, a dreamy spire in the distance.

Urged on by my teachers, I had applied to take natural sciences at Cambridge. I do remember that I enjoyed the cut and thrust of my Oxbridge interview. The professors prodded and poked. I ducked and dived. Perhaps a little too much. It was all over in a flash.

This was the time of my bleached-blond psychobilly hair. In the Clarendon club in 1980s Hammersmith, this was *de rigueur*. But in Cambridge it stuck out like an upturned toilet brush. Whether I was wearing my eyeliner during the interview I can't say.

I got a few things wrong that day. I assumed my academic interviewers would stereotype me because of my looks. But it was me who prejudged them, rather than the other way round. My appearance didn't seem to bother them at all. They were interested in finding out what was going on between my pierced earlobes. I'd just moved out of my home after my mum and dad had split up. After my interview, the tutors spoke with me about my personal situation with great sensitivity and care.

My other mistake was to assume I would be tested on how well I could recall the facts and figures I'd crammed into my 17-year-old mind. Wasn't that what all tests were about? In fact it was more a test of mental agility: thinking on your feet, exploring new ideas, seeking connections between old ones. Being the first person in my family to consider higher education, let alone one of the most prestigious universities in the world, the experience was all new to me. I liked it. But as with so many state school students, it caught me completely unawares.

Oxbridge wasn't to be. Within a year I had flunked my A-levels and failed to go to any university. But I learned much that day. Don't fall into preconceptions of people or places you haven't experienced personally – particularly if it prevents you from pursuing something that might change your life! This advice remains true for Oxbridge to this day.

The biggest problem for Cambridge and Oxford is misinformation. Never have two such famous institutions been mired with so many enduring myths and misconceptions.

## Myths

Oxford and Cambridge are different from other universities. They are very old. Communities of students and academics are gathered together in separate colleges, creating clubs for life. Students are taught in small groups. Study is very intensive. Sometimes you're expected to wear gowns and listen to Latin at special ceremonies and formal dinners. There's lots of ancient traditions that are very odd to outsiders.

Oxbridge remains a breeding ground for future elites, from political leaders to Nobel prize winners. Every prime minister since the end of World War Two who has attended an English university has attended just one institution: Oxford. Oxbridge graduates command higher average wages than other graduates. The universities are very hard to get into. They have their own special early deadline for applications. The average Oxbridge applicant has a one in five chance of success.

A big Oxbridge myth is that it is dominated by the privately educated. In 2016, the Sutton Trust found that a fifth of teachers thought fewer than 20% of students at Oxford and Cambridge were from state schools. The actual figure was around 60% at the time. By 2020, it had risen to just under 70%. (State schools make up 93% of all schools.)

And contrary to what many think, studying at Oxbridge doesn't cost more than studying at other universities. The biggest barrier to Oxbridge is getting the grades and applying in the first place.

But perceptions are hard to shift. It's sad that many pupils still suffer from a 'not for the likes of me' attitude. Many could so easily be Oxbridge candidates. It's fine to make a well-informed decision that Oxford and Cambridge is not for you. The UK is blessed with plenty of good degree courses at other prestigious universities. But so often it's unfounded myths that drive students away.

Teachers can also suffer from the 'not for the likes of you' attitude. The Sutton Trust found that less than half of secondary state school teachers would routinely advise their highest-achieving pupils to apply to Oxbridge. Many well-meaning teachers didn't think their students would stand a chance of getting in, and didn't think they would fit in if they got there. The philanthropist and Sutton Trust founder and funder, Sir Peter Lampl, made it his life's work to change all that.

During my 12 years at the Trust I got to know the Oxbridge system well. I stayed at many of the 70 colleges and experienced the ancient customs of college dining.[24] I've had my ears bent by many an Oxbridge expert: past students, eminent professors, admission officers, college presidents, even vice-chancellors. Here I offer my outsider's insider guide to maximising the chances of securing a place at two of the best universities in the world.

# What you can do

Here I provide advice for young people applying to Oxbridge. Your children should be in the driving seat, but they are likely to need lots of help and guidance.

## Talk to admissions tutors

Contact admissions tutors to find out more. Every college has one. They will be busy but keen to help. In Oxbridge of all places I've learned that there's nothing like insider knowledge. With so many things to think about, insiders will know where to focus your energies.

---

24  For Oxbridge insiders it's easy to spot outsiders. It took me a long time to remember to pronounce Magdalen College, Oxford, 'Maudlin'. There is also a separate Magdalene College, Cambridge.

Be careful paying out for advice from companies that claim to be experts on Oxbridge admissions. A huge industry has flourished to help candidates. But beware: often the fees don't confer any advantage.

## Show your love

Remember, your child is auditioning to experts who are leading thinkers in their fields. Your child needs to show a passion for the discipline that these academics have dedicated their lives to. Academics have a much more prominent role in university admissions at Oxbridge than elsewhere.

If your child is studying geography, they need to show their appreciation for oxbow lakes; if they love English literature, they must sing the praises of extended metaphors. If physics is their thing then they should be sure to demonstrate their fascination for wave-particle duality.

Their personal statement should be a love letter to their chosen subject. The Oxbridge universities are very different to Ivy colleges in the United States, which are much more interested in what a student has achieved outside their studies.

## Study traditional subjects

Admission tutors have a greater respect for traditional subjects like English, maths, history, chemistry and French at A-level (see also chapter 18). The reason being, they are subjects that require a lot of analytical thinking. An A-level in general studies or even law may not cut the mustard. The official lists of preferred subjects can be found on the university websites.

## Prepare to debate

If your son or daughter is invited to an interview, the academics will want to see how they can debate and argue on their feet, stretching them out of their comfort zone. The tutors will ask questions they can't prepare for. They want to see the candidates discuss new ideas, make connections and be analytical.

It is not about the student being right or wrong. Remember, the tutors are judging whether they want to teach someone as a future student. There won't be tricks or traps that the myths suggest exist.

It's an academic discussion. Students should read around their subject and come ready to show what they know. Both university websites have detailed advice on how to prepare for the interview.

## Oxford versus Cambridge

The institutions are similar but not the same. While sharing many common elements, selection processes are different in several ways. Research the particular combination of tests, interviews and other steps involved in the application.

Students can only apply to one and not the other. This is an old rule to manage the numbers of applications. Your child must be prepared to justify the choice she or he makes.

## Degree course choice is top priority

Choose the right degree course rather than the right college. The choice of college shouldn't affect your child's chances of securing a place at Oxford or Cambridge.

However, it is worth taking into account how many students a college enrols for each subject. If students cannot decide on their college, they can make an Open College application, where you are automatically assigned to a college. Colleges will know that students have made an open application to them, but they will treat them the same as someone who chose them directly.

## Be prepared to stand by your statement

Students must be comfortable discussing what they have written in their personal statement – especially if they refer to the work of the academic interviewing them! The statement can be used a lot during the interview. Your child should only write about subjects they are comfortable talking about. They should expect to be asked about the topics they have covered, and the wider reading they have done.

## A teacher's reference can make a difference

Don't underestimate the power of a teacher's reference. The hope is that this will be a compelling piece of writing highlighting your child's particular talents in his or her chosen subject, and their suitability for academic study at Oxbridge. The more original and well written it is, the better.

## Check out outreach

Outreach programmes run at Oxford and Cambridge give pupils from less privileged backgrounds a taster of academic life and practical tips on admissions. Students can find out if they qualify, and whether there are any activities near them, by checking the websites of Oxford and Cambridge. The Sutton Trust's residential summer schools can improve chances of getting in. Yet they can be vastly oversubscribed: it's harder to get on the Sutton Trust Cambridge summer school than into Cambridge itself. Your child's school meanwhile may have links with current Oxbridge students who can guide applicants.

## Call the admissions office on A-level results day

When the day comes, it is worth your child ringing the college admissions officers if they have just missed the grade, especially if there are mitigating circumstances. A large number of candidates who do not meet the expected A-level offers still get a place at Oxbridge. In some cases students who originally applied, but didn't get an offer, may find themselves reconsidered if they get higher grades than expected.

Just missing out on a place may feel like a crushing blow at the time. But it isn't a failure. Remember there are many amazing degree courses elsewhere.

### Five bits of advice

- Nothing beats insider knowledge – encourage your child to reach out to admissions tutors to find out more.
- Demonstrating love for the subject is essential – the interview is an audition to experts who have dedicated their lives to it.
- Interviews are a test of how well students can think on their feet, not how much they can remember.
- Choosing the right degree course is more important than choosing the college.
- The more original and well written a teacher's reference is, the better.

# Reading and references

If I could recommend one thing to read it would be:

Rusbridger R. (2015) 'Lifting the lid on Oxford admissions', *Times Higher Education*, 21 December.

Alan Rusbridger, former principal of Lady Margaret Hall, University of Oxford, provides a first-hand account of the Oxford admissions process. The article addresses some of the misconceptions about Oxford as well as describing some processes which are little understood externally. 'The complexity arises from the college system at Oxford,' writes Rusbridger. 'In other universities there would be one central admissions funnel through which all applicants pass. At Oxford there are the faculties as well as thirty colleges (not to mention six permanent private halls) that admit undergraduates.'

## References

151.  *Did you know?*: The Sutton Trust (2016) *Oxbridge admissions research brief.*

152.  *'The average Oxbridge applicant has a one in five chance of success'*: University of Oxford, *Application guide.* University of Cambridge, *Application statistics.*

153.  *Percentages of state school students at Oxford and Cambridge*: The Sutton Trust (2016) *Oxbridge admissions research brief.*

153.  *'less than half of secondary state school teachers would advise their highest-achieving pupils to apply to Oxbridge'*: The Sutton Trust (2016) *Oxbridge admissions research brief.*

## Other general references for this chapter

University of Cambridge, *Application statistics.*

University of Cambridge, *Guide to admissions.*

University of Oxford, *Application guide.*

University of Oxford, *Annual admissions statistical report.*

Bolton, P. (2016) *Oxbridge 'elitism'.* Briefing Paper Number 616. House of Commons Library.

The Sutton Trust (2011) *Degrees of success: university chances by individual school.*

# 20. Life skills for job hunting

**Did you know?**

In 2017, 37% of men aged 18 to 34 in the UK lived with their parents.

**Key takeaways**

- Parents are ideally suited to help their adult children make their first steps on the career ladder.
- Employees will be even more dependent on essential life skills – such as confidence, resilience and networking – in the tech-dominated workplace of the future.
- Postgraduate degrees are worth exploring: good ones are linked with much higher lifetime earnings.

## Boomerang generation

In times past, one of the most traumatic experiences for parents was dropping their children off at university for the first time. It feels like a symbolic moment: the end of their childhood. And goodbyes can be brutally short. Most will want to be rid of you as soon as possible to start their new lives on campus. After 18 long years of being together, the separation can be over in minutes. Many parents sob during the journey back home.

But remember, they'll be back. In the modern parenting era, the emotionally draining college drop-off has become just another staging post in a far longer child-rearing journey. Studies show that parents' involvement is extending further and further into their children's lives – to maturity and beyond.

In the UK, the boomerang generation reverses a post-war trend that was seeing successive cohorts of children leave their family homes barely after they had turned into teenagers. The era of rising rents and increasing competition over jobs has put paid to all that. Every year, surveys report rising proportions of 20- and 30-year-olds staying at home with their parents. In 2017, the Office for National Statistics found that 37% of men aged 18 to 34 had yet to move out. In academic speak, multigenerational co-residence is becoming the new norm.

## Nurturing essential life skills

Parents are ideally suited to help their adult children in this new phase of co-habitation. In the tech-dominated workplace of the future, employees will be even more dependent on essential life skills – like confidence, resilience and networking – precisely because they are human traits. Having spent a large chunk of their lifetimes at work, parents know only too well what things make a difference in the real world: how good you are with people, how much you can learn on the job, how far you can stick at something. As your children make their way in their fledgling careers, your insights can turn their small steps into great strides.

The irony of the ever-escalating educational arms race is that life skills have become more of an advantage for those who develop them. Most school pupils and university students get little time to nurture their other selves with so much time spent revising for academic tests. Increasing numbers of A grades and first-class degrees mean that non-academic characteristics distinguish a few stand-out candidates from the rest. Job interviews rely on candidates having a mix of technical knowledge and interpersonal skills.

## What you can do

### Getting work experience

Getting work experience is an essential step in the world of job hunting. Not only does it equip children with much-needed life skills, it gives them a sense of self-esteem as well. For future employers, it demonstrates initiative.

Parents can help in so many ways. You can support children to find part-time jobs when they're able to. These can be invaluable experiences, as well as generating some cash. Urge them to volunteer for work experience even if it isn't paid, as long as it's worthwhile (and they're not being exploited). I know many parents who have paid their older children to do jobs around the house, from decorating to dog walking; anything to get them into a working mindset. It's important to instil a work ethic and develop a sense of independence.

Can you exploit your own networks to enable your children to apply for opportunities in something they're interested in, whether it is a few weeks' work experience, an internship or even a permanent job? That opening may only be one person away, whether it is a work colleague, friend, friend of a friend, or neighbour. Try to strike the right balance: make initial introductions, but then hand over to your child to seal the deal.

## Get them networking

It's worth stressing the importance of networking. We all know it's true: success is down as much to who you know as to what you know. But we also know you have to be prepared to put in the hours. Studies have confirmed the link between networking and various measures of career success.

Encourage your children to introduce themselves to anyone who might be able to help them. People can only say no. And there are so many people who are waiting to be asked, and would gladly help out. Could someone act as a mentor or sponsor for them in their chosen career? If they have started work, can they seek feedback from work colleagues on how they can improve? Urge them to explore social media sites such as LinkedIn to expand their professional networks.

Networking can be gruelling work: hanging around evening events when you'd rather be at home, introducing yourself to people who don't really want to speak with you. But nurturing relationships with senior colleagues is important if you want to climb the career ladder. The power of networking is the multiplier effect: it's not just about the immediate person you're speaking with, but all the others they can introduce you to as well.

## Help them to work smart

Encouraging your children to work hard seems like such obvious advice. But it's really working smart that matters most: working hard at the right time. Careers can turn on key moments. A successful journalist I once knew enjoyed a highly successful career after getting through one make-or-break moment. She had been a complete outside bet to secure a post on a national newspaper. But she spent weeks researching the biographies and written work of the people interviewing her. She knew more about their views than they did themselves. She got the job and went on to be a national TV journalist. She worked hard on the right things at the right time.

I've seen this countless times, whether it's preparing for interviews, writing application letters, or going for promotion: it's not so much working hard that matters but working smart.

At these key moments, stress the importance of preparation to your children. As the old saying goes, prior preparation and practice prevents poor performance. As my former boss, Sir Peter Lampl, founder and chairman of the Sutton Trust, has said, you then 'give yourself a chance to get lucky'.

## Adopting a confident mindset

I advise students to be unashamedly assertive in their lives. As a former CEO bombarded with applications, I've seen it from the other side: no matter how pushy they think they are, there are other people who have asked for more. Sadly, just keeping your head down and working hard won't get you noticed.

Can you help your children adopt a positive attitude? I'm convinced it can make a big difference. As the former England football manager, Terry Venables, once remarked: in life, the very worst regret you can have when you're older is not failing at something, but not trying in the first place – and never knowing what might have been. 'Fake it till you make it,' one student once said to me. I found it to be very good advice.

## Embracing rejection

Graduates, fresh out of college, can find rejection a new and unsettling experience. Tell them that all successful people are rejected many times. That's what made them. They bounced back stronger. It's part of the journey.

If it's possible we should always try to find out why we didn't make the grade, pass the interview or get the job. Receiving feedback enables us to learn for the next time.

Grit, or perseverance, is a stronger predictor of lifetime success than innate talent, according to the American psychologist Angela Duckworth. Duckworth argues that by exhibiting grit themselves, parents can bring forth grit in their own children.[25] But other researchers have argued that what matters most is finding something you are passionate about in the first place. We persevere because we've found something we believe is worth investing in. Help your children find their passion.

## Consider postgraduate possibilities

Finally, consider whether further study might be the best option. A degree is no longer the automatic passport to a well-paid job it once was; a master's qualification or PhD is often required to distinguish you from other candidates. It pays to be a postgraduate. A graduate with a master's will earn on average over £200,000 more

---

25    You can even take a test called The Grit Scale to find out how gritty you are.

over a 40-year working life than a graduate with a plain old bachelor's degree.[26] Many are gateway courses to professions.

But be careful: if you thought choosing a degree was a risky venture, it goes to new levels for postgraduate study. For one, it is a completely different academic market: there are many excellent specialist master's degrees offered by universities outside the traditional academic elites. There is no central application process as there is for undergraduate degrees. And your children will have to fork out to pay fees as well as take out loans. Earnings from different postgrad degrees vary enormously.

But they can be good investments if you do your homework. If your children know what type of job they want to go into, people in the industry will know what postgraduate degrees are worthwhile. Sponsorship possibilities or 'learn why you earn' routes may be options. For all these reasons and more, it is critical you do your research. Get your children to look at courses on the internet, ask former students about their experiences and outcomes, and talk to people already working in the field.

Ensure they find something genuinely worthwhile. The worst thing they can do is to use further study as a way of avoiding the world of work. Many postgraduates find themselves being rejected for jobs they are overqualified for.

## Five bits of advice

- Use your networks to secure your children work experience: it will equip them with life skills and boost their confidence.

- Emphasise the importance of networking: in your early career, who you know is more important than what you know.

- Help them to adopt a confident mindset, treating rejection as a learning experience on their career journey.

- Encourage them to work smart, putting in the hours when it matters most: it gives them a chance to get lucky.

- Do your homework when helping them to choose a postgraduate degree – this is essential.

---

26   In 1996, just 1% of 26–60 year olds in the workforce held a postgraduate degree; in 2015 this had risen to 13%. Over two million working adults had a master's degree or PhD.

# Reading and references

If I could recommend one thing to read it would be:

Duckworth, A. (2016) *Grit: the power of passion and perseverance*. Scribner.

Psychologist Angela Duckworth argues that the secret to outstanding achievement is not talent but a blend of passion and persistence she calls grit. 'Interests are not discovered through introspection. Instead, interests are triggered by interactions with the outside world,' writes Duckworth. 'The process of interest discovery can be messy, serendipitous, and inefficient. This is because you can't really predict with certainty what will capture your attention and what won't... Without experimenting, you can't figure out which interests will stick, and which won't.'

## References

159.  *Did you know?*: Office for National Statistics (2019) *Milestones: journeying into adulthood.*

159.  *'parents' involvement is extending further'*: Elliot Major, L. and Machin, S. (2018) *Social mobility and its enemies*. Penguin.

160.  *'37% of men aged 18 to 34 had yet to move out'*: Office for National Statistics (2019) *Milestones: journeying into adulthood.*

160.  *'employees will be even more dependent on essential life skills'*: Deming, D. (2017) 'The growing importance of social skills in the labor market', *Quarterly Journal of Economics*, 132, pp.1593–1640.

      See also: Gutman, L. M. and Schoon, I. (2013) *The impact of non-cognitive skills on outcomes for young people: a literature review.* Education Endowment Foundation/Cabinet Office.

161.  *The link between networking and career success*: Forret, M. L. and Dougherty, T. W. (2001) 'Correlates of networking behavior for managerial and professional employees', *Group and Organization Management*, 26, pp.283–311.

      See also: Wolff, H-G. and Moser, K. (2009) 'Effects of networking on career success: a longitudinal study', *The Journal of Applied Psychology*, 94, pp.196–206.

162.  *'in life, the very worst regret you can have when you're older is not failing at something, but not trying in the first place'*: Venables, T. (2014) *Born to manage: the autobiography.* Simon & Schuster.

162.  *Grit is a stronger predictor of lifetime success*: Duckworth, A. (2016) *Grit: the power of passion and perseverance*. Scribner.

See also: Duckworth, A. L., Peterson, C., Matthews, M. D. and Kelly, D. R. (2007) 'Grit: Perseverance and passion for long term goals', *Journal of Personality and Social Psychology*, 92, pp.1087–1101.

162.  *'what matters most is finding something you are passionate about'*: Mehta, J. (2015) 'The problem with grit', *Education Week*.

See also: Crede, M., Tynan, M. and Harms, P. (2017) 'Much ado about grit: a meta-analytic synthesis of the grit literature', *Journal of Personality and Social Psychology*, 113 (3), pp.492–511.

162.  *'A graduate with a master's will earn on average over £200,000 more'*: Elliot Major, L. and Machin, S. (2018) *Social mobility and its enemies*. Penguin.

See also: Lindley, J. and Machin, S. (2016) 'The rising postgraduate pay premium', *Economica*, 83, pp.281–306.

See also: Buscha, F., Britton, J., Dickson, M., van der Erve, L., Vignoles, A., Walker, I., Waltmann, B. and Zhu, Y. (2020) *The earnings returns to postgraduate degrees in the UK*. Department for Education.

# 21. What's fair game?

**Did you know?**

One in three parents say they know families who have used ethically dubious tactics to win a school place for their children.

**Key takeaways**

- An increasingly competitive education system is creating ever more temptations for parents to cheat to get their children ahead.
- Parents hold very different views about what is fair game in school and university admissions.
- Watch out that your children's success doesn't become a marker of your own social status. Cheating helps no-one.

## In the dock

In 2019, FBI agents charged 50 parents with breaking the law. It made for an unlikely line-up of villains in the dock: doctors, lawyers, and CEOs. They included Felicity Huffman, whose main claim to fame up to that point was to star in the TV show *Desperate Housewives*.

'In my desperation to be a good mother I talked myself into believing that all I was doing was giving my daughter a fair shot,' pleaded Felicity Huffman to her prosecutors. In truth, the actress hadn't been fair at all. She had paid $15,000 to boost the score of her daughter Sophia's college admission test. That was enough to turn the official or 'proctor' trusted with ensuring students didn't cheat into a cheat himself. In the hyper-competitive race to get elite colleges places, Sophia had been handed a golden ticket that catapulted her to the front of the admissions queue. Huffman was sentenced to a 14-day prison sentence, and remains one of the few parents to publicly admit their guilt.

At the heart of the biggest scandal in the history of college admissions was a corrupt college counsellor named William (Rick) Singer.[27] Singer pocketed a total of $25 million to bribe college coaches, boost test scores, and fabricate CVs to guarantee 'side door entry' into prestigious universities such as Yale, Stanford, and the University of Southern California.

Singer was a highly skilled manipulator, preying on parents' obsessions with looking successful to the outside world. 'The parents are applying to college, and the kid is the vehicle through which they apply,' Perry Kalmus, a college counsellor (not involved in the scandal), told the subsequent 2021 Netflix documentary. 'If you're a parent and you didn't go to Harvard, this is your chance to now go to Harvard ... in your warped mind.'

On one level, this was a story about America's increasingly detached entitled elites – sun-lit Ivy League campuses and Californian scheming.[28] But the Huffman affair also highlighted universal questions for us all.

The uncomfortable truth is that we're all capable of lying and cheating to get our children ahead in the educational arms race.

It's easy for parents to lose perspective when trying to do the best for their children. The primal drive to ensure our offspring prosper in life is so strong it can slip into excessive, immoral and even illegal behaviour. We are all vulnerable to viewing our children's success as a marker of our own social status – while convincing ourselves that we are acting in the best interests of our sons and daughters.

On this side of the pond there is lots of denial about cheating in school admissions. In one survey, one in three parents said they knew families who had used ethically dubious tactics to win a school place. One in six parents were able to be more specific: they knew other families who had falsely used a relative's address to get their children into a local school.

Yet only one in fifty of the wealthiest parents surveyed confessed to having actually used a relative's address themselves. Admissions over admissions have fallen over recent years, probably because parents are more aware than ever that it is frowned upon by others.

---

27   Singer pleaded guilty in a federal court in Boston to fraud, racketeering, money laundering, and obstruction of justice

28   In 2021, the affair was the subject of the Netflix documentary *Operation Varsity Blues*.

These may not be illegal activities, but they are certainly unfair. I've witnessed the dubious tactics first hand. Teachers at our local school noticed a stream of new families notifying the school office of 'a change in home address' soon after their children had started at the school. It soon became clear they had rented flats nearby temporarily to pretend that was their permanent home to secure their children school places.

The scam prompted a huge controversy among local residents. Many had lived in the area for decades. They felt their children had been unfairly elbowed out. The illusion of an orderly British society where everyone plays by the rules had been shattered.

Council officials vowed to tighten up the school admissions rules. But the ever resourceful cheats were already one step ahead of the admissions police. Parents arriving in the area had identified a new loophole: paying private doctors to provide evidence for 'exceptional medical or social reasons'. It was another way of ensuring that their children would get to the front of the admissions queue. Once term began, ailments, just like addresses, would mysteriously disappear. The middle classes always find a way.

The education system is set up to encourage us to fight it out against each other. Schools and universities operate in a marketplace, and we parents have become avid fee-paying consumers. In theory this makes parents feel more empowered, with a greater say in their child's educational experience. But in reality many parents feel overwhelmed and resort to unethical behaviours.

Clear offside rules we can all abide by don't exist. What is completely justifiable for some people, is a flagrant breach of the rules for others. And many of us are in denial. Parents will scurry up to the moral uplands at the slightest suggestion they have broken any rules. School admissions, like religion and politics, is a no-go topic at the dinner table (but always seems to surface after a few drinks).

## Fine lines

It can also be a fine line between what is considered wrong and right. Have you ever stretched the truth just a little to ensure that your son or daughter gets ahead? Have you helped them to write their personal statement for a university application? Have you 'rediscovered' your faith and attended church for a few months so they can be admitted into the local church school? Have you done some light editing to improve your child's essay so they get better marks in their exam?

There doesn't seem to be an age limit for these undercover interventions. Many parents have confided to me that they have given their children a helping hand. For some it stops at the primary school homework stage; for others it extends to contributing to research dissertations for university degrees.

I was once asked as an education expert to comment on a BBC News story about rising numbers of pupils qualifying for extra time in their exams. They had found that one in five private school pupils received extra time compared with only one in eight pupils in state schools. Pupils can be awarded 25% extra exam time if they are diagnosed with having dyslexia, developmental coordination disorders such as dyspraxia, attention deficit hyperactivity disorder (ADHD), or other conditions.

Private school heads were accused of gaming the exam system to boost their results. Yet this wasn't necessarily the case. They may have just had better resources to identify students who had genuine special educational needs.

I would strongly urge all parents to consider asking for a diagnosis of their child if there are consistent signs that they may have a learning need. They are difficult to detect as so many possible signs (such as being distracted or disorganised) are part of normal childhood.[29] Many teachers are not trained to spot conditions. Many children will mask conditions such as autism. Far too often, they get missed and picked up too late to address children's needs. The whole aim of this book is to empower parents to fight their child's corner when needed, to question teachers where appropriate, and to appeal against a decision when there is reason to do so.

But in the educational arms race, it's difficult to distinguish the difference between sticking up for your educational rights and gaming the system to gain unfair advantage.

Another topic of academic debate is the proliferation of 'smart pills' used to enhance exam performance. Medicines such as Modafinil, Ritalin and Adderall are prescribed to improve concentration for pupils with conditions such as ADHD. But the growing numbers of middle-class parents clamouring for education psychiatrists to prescribe the drugs are raising suspicions that this is more about gaming test scores than safeguarding the wellbeing of their children. Some see a day when schools and universities will have to introduce drug testing during exams.

The use of drugs to boost mental performance is booming across the world. And the UK has witnessed one of the biggest increases in so-called pharmacological cognitive enhancement. In 2015, one in twenty survey participants had used smart drugs; in 2017, just under one in four (23%) had done so. Only the Netherlands and the United States had higher rates of use.

---

29  The percentage of pupils with special educational needs (SEN) in England was 15.5% in 2020 – just under one in six pupils – according to official statistics from the Department for Education.

Cheating in education is on the rise in general, driven by new opportunities the new technological age brings. Rising numbers of pupils are caught each year smuggling mobile phones into exam halls for their GCSE and A-level exams. University authorities meanwhile are facing an uphill struggle clamping down on students using paid-to-order essays in a burgeoning industry of essay mill websites. It's what comes with high-stakes testing. Research shows that students are more likely to cheat in classes that emphasise tests and grades rather than learning and mastering content.

On occasion, teachers can also be implicated. In 2017, a government inquiry was launched to investigate accusations that teachers at Eton and other leading public schools had passed information to pupils about their upcoming exams. The scandal prompted resignations at the schools and calls for tighter rules under which teachers work as examiners writing and reviewing question papers. Announcing the inquiry, the Schools Minister Nick Gibb warned that 'cheating of any kind is unacceptable'. But mounting pressure on teachers and their students is leading many to break the rules.

## The costs of cheating

What is certain is that parents will be confronted with ever more temptations as the competition in schools, colleges and universities intensifies. The pressure seems to ratchet up with every passing academic year. As with any sport, it's fine to push the game's rules to the limits, but very different when you cross the line and cheat.

You will recognise the warning signs of over-competitive tendencies. Are you finding yourself spending more time telling others that your children have come top of the class, or come first in the school race? When your friends mention their children, do you find yourself not listening and just thinking about what you can tell them about yours? Is there anything you've done that you aren't able to tell your children about?

Ensure the choices you make are about them, not you. How much are you genuinely listening to your children's views, when helping them to choose a degree or apprenticeship or school subject? It's important to respect our own children's choices, particularly as they get older, and not impose our own ones.

And be slow to judge others. In my experience, we're all guilty of double standards. It takes a strong person to turn the spotlight on themselves. Remember that what you count as unfair behaviour may not be the same from someone else's perspective.

The school or university your children attend is not the be-all and end-all of their lives. As we have shown, the extra benefit added by one school compared with another is much smaller than you think. Our ultimate goal is to nurture our children to be their own independent thinkers equipped to prosper and enjoy their own lives. Reflect on this before it's too late. However much you can justify cheating to yourself, it's unlikely to be setting a good example for your children.

It was young people who were the biggest victims in the Huffman affair: those elbowed out of college places they would have won if it had been a fair competition; and the sons and daughters who were apparently unaware that their test scores had been artificially inflated. Tragically, their parents' actions revealed a lack of self-esteem that was being passed on from one generation to the next. It later emerged that many children would have done well on their admissions tests and won other college places deservedly. Family relationships will be left scarred for life. Cheating is not good for anyone.

Excessive parenting may do more harm than good for us and our children; ill-judged parenting damages children permanently. The good parent educators empower their children through education. The bad parent educators seek to empower themselves through their children's education.

My advice is simple: try to keep a cool head, focus on your children's true needs, and don't cheat.

# Reading and references

If I could recommend one thing to read it would be:

Golden, D. and Burke, D. (2019) 'The unseen student victims of the varsity blues college-admissions scandal', *The New Yorker*.

An article on the many personal victims of the 2019 US college-admissions scandal. These included many deserving students who aspired to attend colleges but were rejected despite their stronger credentials. 'The elite colleges involved have portrayed themselves as helpless victims,' the authors argue. 'In reality, they created the conditions for Singer's scheme, from the lower admissions standards for athletes to the ever-increasing selectivity that ratchets up parents' desperation.'

## References

167.   *Did you know?*: Montacute, R. and Cullinane, C. (2018) *Parent power 2018: how parents use financial and cultural resources to boost their children's chances of success.* The Sutton Trust.

167.   *The US college-admissions scandal*: BBC News (2019) 'Felicity Huffman handed prison time over college admissions scandal', 13 September.

       See also: Jones, E. (2021) 'Operation varsity: how the rich and famous cheated the US university system', *BBC News*, 18 March.

168.   *Parents knew families who had used ethically dubious tactics*: Montacute, R. and Cullinane, C. (2018) *Parent power 2018: how parents use financial and cultural resources to boost their children's chances of success.* The Sutton Trust.

170.   *'one in five private school pupils received extra time'*: Bateman, T. (2017) 'Independent school students gain extra time for exams', *BBC News*, 10 February.

170.   *Smart drugs rates of use*: Maier, L. J., Ferris, J. A. and Winstock, A. R. (2018) 'Pharmacological cognitive enhancement among non-ADHD individuals: a cross-sectional study in 15 countries', *International Journal of Drug Policy*, 58, pp.104–112.

       See also: Winstock, A. R., Barrett, M. J., Ferris, J. A. and Maier, L. J. (2018) *Global Drug Survey (GDS) 2018: global overview and highlights.*

       See also: Marsh S. (2017) 'Universities must do more to tackle use of smart drugs, say experts', *The Guardian*, 10 May.

171.   *Rising numbers of pupils are caught smuggling mobile phones into exam halls*: Ofqual Official Statistics (2018) *Malpractice in GCSE, AS and A level: summer 2018 exam series.*

171.   *University authorities are facing an uphill struggle clamping down on students using paid-to-order essays*: McCabe, D. L., Butterfield, K. D. and Treviño, L. K. (2017) *Cheating in college: why students do it and what educators can do about it*. John Hopkins University Press.

171.   *'students are more likely to cheat in classes that emphasise tests and grades'*: Anderman, E. M. (2018) 'Why students at prestigious high schools still cheat on exams', *The Conversation*.

See also: Elliot Major, L. and Weiner, J. (2020) 'Rethinking social mobility in education: looking through the lens of professional capital', *Journal of Professional Capital and Community*.

171.   *Government inquiry into cheating teachers*: Yorke, H. (2017) 'Government orders investigation into public school cheating scandal as regulator considers change in rules', *The Daily Telegraph*, 31 August.

### Other general references for this chapter

Elliot Major, L. and Machin, S. (2018) *Social mobility and its enemies*. Penguin.

Golden, D. (2005) *The price of admission: how America's ruling class buys its way into elite colleges — and who gets left outside the gates*. Crown Publishing.

Kirby, P. (2016) *Shadow schooling: private tuition and social mobility in the UK*. The Sutton Trust.

West, A. and Hind, A. (2006) 'Selectivity, admissions and intakes to "comprehensive" schools in London, England', *Educational Studies*, 32 (2), pp.145–155.

# 22. The good parent educator quiz

Have you got what it takes to be a good parent educator? Find out by answering ten questions to test your knowledge of the topics covered throughout the book. Testing what you know through a quiz is one of the best ways of remembering things. These questions are intended to consolidate some of the points made throughout the book. There may be more than one correct answer, or no correct answers at all. Answers are given at the end.

## Questions

1.  30 minutes every day is enough to get benefits from:
    A.  Reading with your children
    B.  Regular sport or exercise
    C.  Homework for an 11-year-old
    D.  One-to-one tutoring

2.  What is the most likely sign of a good school?
    A.  Small class sizes
    B.  Uniforms
    C.  New buildings
    D.  A charismatic headteacher

3.  Pupils spend as much as 80% of their time in class:
    A.  Pretending to listen
    B.  Talking to their classmates
    C.  Listening to their teacher
    D.  Daydreaming

4. What's the best way to improve your children's progress at school?
   A. Getting more marks from teachers
   B. Getting more homework
   C. Getting them in the top sets
   D. Changing schools

5. What's the best way to revise?
   A. Going over texts and highlighting key passages
   B. Constantly switching between completely different subjects
   C. Going over material in one go
   D. Testing yourself by doing quizzes

6. What's the best way to praise your children?
   A. Tell them that they are very clever
   B. Congratulate them on their accomplishment
   C. Praise their efforts
   D. Compare them with what other children have done

7. You can be sure you have a good tutor if they:
   A. Charge more money per hour
   B. Are a former teacher
   C. Are a current teacher
   D. Are a top university graduate

8. Someone who gets a university degree earns more than:
   A. Someone who leaves school and goes straight into a job
   B. Someone who takes an apprenticeship
   C. Someone who drops out of university
   D. Someone who goes on to take a postgraduate degree

9. Which of these A-level subjects tend to be preferred by highly selective universities?
   A. Law
   B. Business
   C. Psychology
   D. English

10. Which of these is breaking education rules?
    A. Renting a flat near a sought-after school
    B. Attending church to get into a faith school
    C. Helping your children with their university applications
    D. Taking a pill to enhance exam performance

# Answers

1. Yes to all of these, with some provisos for c). A daily routine of reading for young children should last for at least 20 minutes. Any less than this, and the benefits diminish. It is recommended that children do at least 60 minutes of exercise daily. But benefits can be achieved through 30 minutes per day. Researchers meanwhile suggest a daily maximum of 60 minutes of homework for 11-year-olds. But this is only useful if homework provides genuine feedback that moves children's learning on. In schools, one-to-one tutoring is often organised in daily sessions of 30 minutes over a school term. Daily private tutoring may be a good option in the run up to exams.

   Remember the universal educational law: do a little a lot regularly. This applies whether children are revising for exams or practising sport or learning a musical instrument.

2. None of these factors will tell you for sure. Distinguishing between a good school and a not so good school is harder than it seems.

   Smart school uniforms or shiny new buildings do not, by themselves, improve academic results. Reducing class sizes by two or three pupils won't have much impact either; it's only when classes are very small (around 15 pupils) that teachers change what they do. Studies have also struggled to single out a 'headteacher effect'.

   The key question for the school is how is it improving teaching throughout its classrooms. Reading Ofsted reports and league tables can generate some good questions. Talk to current pupils and parents. How do they look after the wellbeing of pupils, and what do they offer in arts and sports?

3. The answer is a) although it could be d) as well. Graham Nuthall's research exposes the real world of the classroom. Even the best teachers aren't able to tell what pupils are thinking most of the time. One of his studies found that pupils spend 80% of their time in class pretending to listen. Engaging pupils in individualised feedback is one of the best ways of improving their progress.

Nuthall also found that 80% of the feedback pupils receive is from fellow pupils, and 80% of this is wrong. He also discovered the 'rule of three': students need to be taught something three times before it embeds in their long-term memory.

4. None of these are guaranteed to improve a child's progress, but b) homework, done well, can improve outcomes for secondary school students. The problem with most marking is that most of it doesn't include information that can move learning on for pupils. For similar reasons, homework at primary school has little impact.

   Getting into a top set also may not help. The big-fish-little-pond effect shows that students ranked lowly in top academic sets suffer from lower academic confidence than similarly achieving students in lower sets. Changing schools will only have a marginal effect on academic progress. Better progress comes from having better teachers and putting more effort in.

5. The answer is d). Highlighting text might give you a sense of accomplishment, but it doesn't help to transfer the words into your memory. The same is true for re-reading and summarising.

   Revising a little a lot over time is a much more effective approach than doing a lot at one time. Spacing is effective because it allows you to forget information and re-learn it. Alternating between types of questions and topics within a subject is a promising revision strategy. But switching between completely different subjects in a short space of time may just confuse learners.

   Testing yourself is one of the most effective learning approaches we know. It forces you to try to generate answers. Simply explaining something to yourself also helps. Every time you look up an answer you rob yourself of a learning opportunity.

6. The answer is c). It is better to praise effort rather than accomplishment. This encourages a growth mindset, which is associated with better outcomes. Just telling children they are clever doesn't incentivise effort and provides little information for why they have done well. It's best to focus on improving personal bests, rather than comparing with others. Praise needs to be sparing and specific to be meaningful.

7. The best answers are b) or c), although you can never truly be sure of the effectiveness of a tutor until you have tried them out. One-to-one school tutoring programmes involving trained teachers have twice the effect of those deploying teaching assistants or volunteers.

   Students or graduates are a riskier bet, but can be a highly effective and cheaper option, particularly if they have been trained. Private tutoring is an unregulated industry; there are no guarantees irrespective of how much you're paying.

8. It depends! Extra earnings from degrees compared with school leavers have held up remarkably well despite increasing numbers of students. But the average figures mask wide variation. For some degrees, graduates earn less than non-graduates. Many degree-level apprentices meanwhile earn more over their lifetimes than some graduates. A graduate with a master's degree will earn on average more than a graduate, but again there is wide variation.

   It's important that you do your own research to find out what the employment prospects are for specific courses.

9. The answer is d). Of course it depends on the degree, and each university is slightly different. But as a general rule, selective universities tend to prefer traditional A-level subjects including biology, chemistry, physics, English, geography, history and maths. They are less keen on more vocational A-level subjects such as law, accounting and business.

   Two in five university students said they would have made better choices if they'd had better information and advice at school. Official lists of preferred subjects can be found on university websites.

10. It depends exactly on how you've done these things. There's nothing wrong with renting a flat near a school. But using a false address to get your children into a local school is against admissions rules. Meanwhile, some church schools are trying to clamp down on cynical parents rediscovering their faith temporarily for the sole purpose of getting their children admitted into the school.

    Of course parents help their children navigate the bafflingly complex world of university admissions. But it doesn't help anyone in the long run if your son or daughter's personal statement has been completely crafted by you or others. Medicines can be prescribed to improve concentration for pupils and students with conditions such as ADHD. But there are concerns that the pills are now being used purely to boost test scores.

People vary in where they draw the line of what is fair. But if you are tempted to cheat, reflect on the damage it may cause you and your children. It's unlikely to boost their self-esteem in the long run. Is it more about your own status than their futures?